To Maddie—

with my best
wishes —

Montrew Dunham

ABIGAIL'S SECRET

By Montrew Dunham
Illustrated by Cathy Morrison

NEW CENTURY PUBLISHING

Library of Congress
Cataloging-in-Publication Data
Dunham, Montrew
Abigail's Secret
by Montrew Dunham

ISBN   978-0-9822344-8-8

new century
PUBLISHING
1040 E. 86th Street, Suite 42A
Indianapolis, IN 46240

Dedication

To my dear friends,
Louise, Doris and Harriette

Table of Contents

Chapter One

All of the family remained seated around the dining room table, even though dinner was over. Father, at the head of the table, looked very serious. There was no hint of a twinkle in his brown eyes, and his mouth was stern.

Eleven-year-old Abigail looked around at each one of the family. At the other end of the table Mother sat straight and tall. Her deep blue eyes were clear and bright, but her mouth was drawn firm without a trace of her usual smile. Aunt Hester, Uncle George, and Cousin Gloria sat in a tight row together on one side of the table. Gram sat to Father's right on the other side of the table and then Abigail, her sister Caroline, and her brother Robert.

It was an unusual Friday evening. Usually, dinner on Friday evenings was lively, with story telling and laughter. Gram often told stories of the olden days, and Father would laugh when she told stories about him as a little boy. Mother would ask Caroline about school, and Robert would talk about the basketball games and who was winning. Uncle George would tell about the people he had talked with when he was looking for a job, and Aunt Hester would tell how she was going to decorate their house when they moved. Sometimes it seemed everyone would talk at once. But they all listened, and they all laughed together at each other and at themselves. Tonight there was no laughter.

Almost all week had been unusual. Franklin Delano Roosevelt was inaugurated as President of the United States just last Saturday on March 4, 1933, which had seemed so very special. And then the next day, he proclaimed that all the banks in the country were to be closed. A bank holiday!

Abigail frowned as she thought about it…a holiday had a good sound…but for them there was nothing good about this holiday. It meant that they had no money!

Everyone sat in silence for such a long time that it seemed like an eternity, but no one moved to leave the table.

Finally, it was Mother who broke the silence. "We have spent the week worrying about money. We know that somehow we will work things out.

I don't know quite how, but together we will manage."

"We don't have money to buy groceries, to pay the milkman, or the gas bill. The electric bill is overdue, and we are apt to lose the house if we can't pay at least the interest on the mortgage payment," Father said grimly. He shook his head. "I should have put some money aside. I should have made some arrangements!"

"What money…what arrangements!" Mother exclaimed. "We have needed every cent we had!"

"I should have taken some money out of the bank and kept it at home," Father said.

"Samuel! How could you have known that President Roosevelt would close the banks!" Gram interrupted, "I knew I made a mistake when I voted for that man!"

Uncle George shook his head, "Samuel, you have supported us all. I feel terrible that I haven't been able to help."

Aunt Hester turned to Uncle George and said in a tight voice, "You couldn't help losing your job in this awful depression. Where will it all end?"

"We need to look at what we have," Mother said in a no-nonsense tone. "We have a comfortable house with enough coal in the coal cellar to keep us warm all winter."

"If the winter doesn't last too long!" Father interrupted.

Mother lifted her chin a little higher, "And, we have plenty of food canned from the garden."

"Such as it is," Caroline said under her breath.

Mother's blue eyes were bright and cold as she looked directly at Caroline. "Caroline, please clear the table." And then she turned to Abigail, "and you help your sister."

Abigail looked at Gloria who smiled her sickening sweet smile at Abigail and didn't move. Gloria's mother never told her to do anything, and she never did...do anything!

Abigail's heart was pounding. She didn't know when to share her secret. She put her napkin on the table and quickly slipped the package from under it and put it on her chair behind her as she got up. Gram glanced at her quickly, and Abby knew that Gram had seen. Abigail didn't know what to do next, so she just got up and started to take the dishes from the table.

Caroline took a tray from the sideboard and began to stack the dirty dishes on it to carry to the kitchen. Abigail took what she could carry and placed them on the kitchen sink. Caroline came right behind her with her fully loaded tray. "How dumb...why didn't you get a tray and bring a full load, instead of making a dozen trips?" Caroline was 18, going to college at Madame Blaker's Teachers College, and she thought she was so smart…like she knew everything!

Abigail felt a little smug. Just wait until Caroline found out that she didn't know everything!

As she went back to get more dishes, though, she did get a tray, and Caroline said, "That's more like it."

Abigail couldn't help it. She stuck her tongue out at her sister behind her back. Her mother saw her and frowned.

Caroline was the oldest…and the smartest… and the prettiest. She had that curly black hair, which always looked just right, and her eyes were so blue. And when she smiled, which wasn't often, she had dimples. It just wasn't fair! Abigail had straight brown hair, and although she smiled a lot, no dimples. Robert and Abigail looked more alike, although he was 14 and so big, almost as tall as their father.

Even though the table was cleared, no one had yet started to leave. Abigail slipped back into her chair and carefully put her package on her lap.

Gram cleared her throat as she took an envelope from her lap and laid it on the table.

"Samuel, this isn't much, but I would like you to take this money from my sugar bowl to help out."

Father said in a sad voice, "Oh, Mother, I can't take that…"

"Nonsense! We are a family, and we all work together to meet our problems," Gram said quickly.

Everyone knew that Gram saved what little money she could and put it in her sugar bowl for minor emergencies.

And this was no minor emergency! Abigail's father had not lost his job, but almost everyone else had. Uncle George had lost his job and could not find another, and when they ran out of money, Uncle George, Aunt Hester, and Gloria had come to live with them.

Abigail's friend Mary Margaret's father had lost his job, too, and Mary Margaret's sister Cecilia and her husband had moved back home to help pay the bills.

Samuel Graham was an insurance agent, and although he still had his job, he earned very little because people could not afford to pay for insurance.

Abigail took a deep breath. It was now time. She took the package from her lap and placed it on the table before her. Conversation stopped, and everyone looked at her. Carefully she unwrapped the package to reveal a small stack of crumpled dollar bills, and she shoved the stack to her father as she said, "This is to help." She looked at her father and then her mother for approval.

"What is this?" Her father looked at the package and then at Abigail as if he couldn't believe what he was seeing.

Mother leaned forward to look squarely at Abigail as she asked sharply, "Where did you get this money?"

"How much is there?" Robert asked.

Father leafed through the money hastily. "There are 20 dollars! Abigail, where did you get this money?"

Abigail was taken aback. She had known it would be difficult to explain, but she had expected that they would be so glad to get the money! She asked, "Aren't you glad to have it? Won't it help with the bills we have to pay?"

"Of course, it would help," Father answered, "and we do appreciate having it. But not if I don't know where you got this money, Abigail!"

Abigail swallowed. Her throat felt so dry. This was the hardest part of the secret. She answered half under her breath, "I can't tell."

Father leaned toward her, "I can't hear what you said; speak up!"

"I can't tell!"

"What do you mean, you can't tell! What are you saying, Abigail?" her father demanded.

All eyes were upon Abigail, and it seemed like everyone was shouting at her at once. Gram frowned a little, and she looked at Abigail in a puzzled way, as Robert asked, "Did you find it?" and Aunt Hester said, "You didn't have 20 dollars, did you?" And then Aunt Hester asked Abby's mother, "Did she have any money of her own?" And Caroline answered, "Of course, she doesn't have money like that!"

The more everyone pressed her to tell, the more she shouted, "I can't tell! I promised! I can't! I can't!"

And then Gloria tossed her blond curls, and with great importance interrupted, "I saw her talking to Uncle Mike. I bet he knows!"

Everyone grew silent, and Abigail felt like she was in a spotlight with everyone staring at her. She shouted at Gloria, "He's not your Uncle Mike!"

Gloria shrugged her shoulders and said, "He most certainly is not!"

Father glared at Abigail, as he exclaimed, "Mike! When did you see Uncle Mike? Abigail, go to your room!"

Abigail could not believe her ears. This had not turned out the way she expected at all! She had thought everyone would be so grateful...that she had saved the day...and now...

"Go to your room!"

Abigail felt hot tears coming to her eyes and a big lump in her throat. As she pushed back from the table, she heard Aunt Hester say, "Where would Mike get any money; he must have stolen it!"

Abigail whirled around as she left the room and shouted through her sobs, "He did not!"

Chapter Two

Abigail ran up the stairs and into her bedroom, slammed the door, and fell on her bed. She couldn't help crying. Everybody hated her, and she had just been trying to help! She thought that Mother and Father would be so relieved to have the money, and they would appreciate her so much! And now they were just mad at her. It didn't seem fair! She felt so sorry for herself.

Everything in their family had changed so much. It wasn't even her own room anymore. She had to share with Glor-i-a, who was such a pain. It used to be that it was just Mother and Father and Caroline and Robert…and, of course, Gram. And that was just right…well, and it was okay when Uncle Mike had come to live with them.

Abigail turned over and dried her eyes. It really was kind of fun when Uncle Mike had come. And then at Thanksgiving time Uncle George, Aunt Hester, and Glor-i-a had moved in, and that wasn't fun at all.

It had been the beginning of the change in everything when Uncle Mike had come to stay, although that was really kind of neat.

And then when Mr. and Mrs. Allen, their neighbors across the street, moved from their house, even the neighborhood had changed. Abby turned on her bed and looked out the window. Even with the leaden gray skies she could see the outline of the dark, empty house across the street. And she had a terrible knot in the pit of her stomach as she thought about the terrible things that had gone on in that house.

Abby's smooth brown hair was mussed and tangled from crying into her pillow, and her eyes, usually a clear blue, were dulled to a gray blue from her tears. She roused a bit as she heard the noise of her bedroom door opening. She rolled over to see who was coming in. At first, there was nothing, and then stealthily Justin stuck his black nose in, and then pushed his thick, black furry body through the opening door. His tail was wagging furiously, as he came over to Abby.

Abby leaned over and put her arms around the neck of her dog. And then she felt even sorrier for herself. She couldn't even have Justin in her room any more…not since Gloria had come. Glor-i-a was allergic to dogs…so Justin had to sleep outside in the playhouse!

Abigail was 11 years old, the youngest in her family, although many times she felt older and smarter than 14-year-old Robert, and she definitely knew she had more sense than Caroline, who was 18.

Caroline studied all the time…that is whenever anything needed to be done. She NEVER did the dishes…she always had a paper to write for her classes at Madame Blaker's Teachers College. And when she wasn't studying, she was washing her bee-u-tiful black curly hair… and setting it just so…or ironing her clothes for school or a date.

And that was something else; she was always talking on the phone to some of her friends. Especially Morrison Strawn! Abigail couldn't see why she liked him so much better than Rusty, the iceman. Rusty went to Purdue to study engineering in the winter, but in the summer he drove the ice truck and carried in blocks of ice for peoples' iceboxes. He was just great, and he always gave ice chips to the kids on hot days.

He liked Caroline, although Abby couldn't see why. Caroline went out with him some evenings, but she was never very nice to him. It was easy to see that Caroline liked Morrison better.

Morrison's family was rich. They lived over on Meridian Street, and they had gotten Caroline's name from Madame Blaker's to be a tutor for

Morrison. He went to Wabash College, but he wasn't very smart in math and needed some help so he could pass his examinations in math. So Caroline helped him with his math and earned some money to help pay her tuition at school. And then Morrison asked Caroline to go out with him. And Caroline was so pleased!

Robert wasn't very good at math either, but Caroline never helped him! Robert was very strong, though, and he was very good at football…and baseball. He could hit a ball farther than anybody! Abigail liked Robert most of the time. He did tease sometimes, but he wasn't really mean when he teased her. Gram always made him stop when he got too rough with his teasing.

Abigail stopped in Gram's room almost every night before she went to bed. Gram had a little sitting room that smelled of lavender and peppermint. She always gave Abby a creamy, smooth peppermint drop, and they talked about their days. Abigail told Gram almost everything. She sniffled and wiped her nose on her sleeves as she thought how hard it had been not to tell Gram her secret.

Their house was largish, but now it seemed to be filled to overflowing. It used to be that everyone had his or her own room. There was even a guestroom. Uncle Mike stayed in the guestroom when he came. Robert had the little room; Gram had her little two-room suite; of course, Caroline still had her own room; and Mother and Father were in their room. But when Aunt Hester and Uncle George came, Abigail had to share her room with Gloria, and Aunt Hester and Uncle George took the guestroom, and Uncle Mike had to move up to the attic. And then at Christmastime he had to move out of the attic, but that was another story.

Abigail frowned as she thought about Christmas…but then her thoughts turned to last summer. She thought about before Gloria came, how she and Mary Margaret, her very best friend, used to take their books and go down to the woods in the vacant lot and sit in the cool of the shady trees and read. Sometimes they took their lunches and had a picnic and just talked.

They played in the playhouse. Sometimes they would have tea, which was really lemonade and cookies and invite their friends for afternoon tea. Sometimes they invited the grownups, too. They even stayed overnight in the playhouse, too, and Justin stayed with them because the dark got a little scary. The playhouse had two stories. The first floor was tall enough even Father could stand up, and there was a little ladder stairway to the second floor, and only kids could stand up there, but there was room for two or three kids to sleep. Father had built the playhouse for Caroline when she was a little girl. When she had outgrown it, Robert used it for a clubhouse for his friends. And now it was Abigail's and Justin's since he couldn't sleep in the house anymore.

After dinner in the summertime, she and Mary Margaret played with their friends under the street light in front of the house as the dusk fell into darkness. Sometimes they played hopscotch or red light–green light and watched the trolley cars go clattering past with the bell clanging. And she remembered back to that warm evening last summer, when Uncle Mike had hopped off the trolley car and had come swinging up the sidewalk.

Chapter Three

Abigail thought about that warm summer evening when she and Mary Margaret were sitting on the front steps watching the trolley cars go by. The street light had just come on, and the summer evening was filled with the laughing and shouting of the boys and girls as they played on the corner. Justin was running around, his black fluffy tail wagging happily.

Mary Margaret looked so glum that Abby asked, "What's the matter with you?"

Mary Margaret told her that they might have to move because her father had been laid off from his job.

Shocked, Abigail said, "But where would you move?"

"I don't know," Mary Margaret shrugged. "I don't know where you move when you don't have any money."

Abigail shook her head slowly, "I don't know…but I hope it's close. I just couldn't stand it if you moved far away." Mary Margaret and Abigail were best friends.

At that moment a trolley car screeched to a stop with sparks flying from the metal wheels on the rails. A man got off, and the trolley car started off. Abigail was so surprised when she recognized that the man was her Uncle Mike. She leapt to her feet and ran to meet him. "I didn't know you were coming!"

"Hi, Abby, are the folks inside?" Uncle Mike's red hair gleamed in the evening sunshine, and his face crinkled as he smiled at Abigail.

Abigail nodded yes, and then she asked, "Want me to get them?"

"No, that's all right. I'll just let myself in," Uncle Mike answered.

"O.K." Abby nodded and sat down by Mary Margaret again. It was always fun when Uncle Mike came to visit. He used to come in his big, shiny car, and he often brought candy and gifts when he came, but not for a long time. Recently, he came only on Sundays when Mother invited him for dinner, not on an ordinary weekday night.

Shortly after Uncle Mike went in, Mother came to the door and called, "Abby! Abigail… time to come in!"

"Oh, Mother, it's not dark yet, and Mary Margaret is here," Abigail pleaded.

"You may go out again, until it's dark. But right now come and help. Gram is doing the dishes."

Abigail ran up the porch steps into the house protesting as she went, "It's Caroline's turn to do the dishes."

Mother opened the screen door. Justin tried to squeeze in the door beside Abby, but Mother blocked him with her foot.

"Mother, I did dishes last night...it's not fair!"

Mother agreed, "I know, but Caroline has a paper to write for her college work."

Caroline was sitting at the dining room table with books all around her. Her curling, black hair fell gracefully over her shoulders as she leaned over her work. She didn't even look up.

"Go on now," Mother gave Abigail a soft pat on her back. "It isn't Gram's turn either, you know. She's doing the dishes so I can help your father."

"O.K." Abby said grudgingly, and she ran on to the kitchen past the study where Father and Uncle Mike were sitting as Mother went back in to join them.

Gram smiled her nice grandmotherly smile, handed Abby a dishtowel, and pointed to the clean dishes in the dish rack. "Sorry, Abby…it's you and me for it."

Abigail smiled…she really didn't mind drying dishes with Gram. But it did make her mad that Caroline always got out of doing the dishes. And it seemed lately that Mother was hardly ever in the kitchen for after dinner clean up. She was always in the study with Father.

"Did you know Uncle Mike was coming, Gram?"

Gram just kept on washing the dishes as she replied, "I heard your father mention that he might be coming." And then she said briskly, "Just put the dishes on the table as you dry them, and I'll put them up in the cupboard."

The window over the sink was open, and a pleasant summer breeze blew the curtains back and cooled the kitchen as they worked. It never took long to get the work done with Gram, not like when she and Caroline did the dishes together.

"Abby, are you done yet?" Mary Margaret called from the back screen door.

"Almost," answered Abby as she dried the silverware and placed it in the drawer with rather noisy clinks and clanks as it landed in the silver sections. She looked at Gram who was scrubbing the pots and pans.

Gram smiled. She knew the question before Abby asked, "Can I be done now?"

"Yes, you can be done now!" echoed Gram. It was the question she always got when they got to the pots and pans. "Hang your dishtowel on the rack, and then you may go with Mary Margaret, but remember your mother wants you in the house by dark!"

Abby danced over to give Gram a quick kiss and hug and hurried out the back door with Mary Margaret. They ran down the back walk to the playhouse with Justin right at their heels. They sat down on the little front porch to talk.

Abby wanted to ask Mary Margaret more about her moving. "Where do you think you will move?"

"Daddy is looking for another job, and if he can find one maybe we won't have to move." Mary Margaret's brown eyes were large and solemn, but after a bit she smiled and turned to Abby and said, "Come on, let's go play! It's nearly dark."

They ran down to the corner to play "red light–green light" with the other kids until the darkness fell all around their circle in the streetlight.

They knew it was time to go in even before they heard her mother call, "Abigail!" and before she had a chance to answer Mother called again, "Abigail Graham!"

"Yes, Mother…I'm coming!"

The girls ran down the street. Abby turned

into her walk, and Mary Margaret ran on down to her house.

Mother was waiting at the door for her. "You go on up and get ready for bed now."

"Do I have to? Can't I stay up a little longer?" Abby always asked to stay up a little longer...no matter what time it was. Mother smiled as she shook her head.

"Will you come up to say goodnight, or can I stop in and see Gram for a bit.?"

"I'll be up later, and if you want...and if it's all right with your grandmother, you can stop in her room for a short good night visit."

Abby ran upstairs and knocked on Gram's door, which was open. She stopped to talk with Gram almost every night. She always asked if she could come in, and Gram never said no. Gram smiled pleasantly and said as she always did, "Of course, you can Abigail, come on in."

And they talked and talked. Gram's name was Patience Graham. She was Father's mother and had lived with them as long as Abigail could remember. Abigail told her about Mary Margaret's father, and Gram said that she hoped they would be able to manage someway so that they wouldn't have to move.

Abigail was puzzled and frowned a little as she said, "I wonder why Mother and Father and Uncle Mike are talking so long."

Gram's voice was flat as she said, "I could guess."

"What? What do you think?"

"I think he wants to come here to live," Gram replied.

"To live?" That was a new thought to Abigail. She had never thought about Uncle Mike living at their house. In one way, it might be fun having him here…and yet a little strange. "Why do you think that? Do you think he has lost his job?"

"Yes, I think so…and…" Gram set her mouth firmly and stopped right there as if she had already said too much.

Thoughtfully, Abigail reached into Gram's candy dish and carefully selected a creamy peppermint. She popped it into her mouth and enjoyed the lovely minty flavor trickling down her throat. And then Abigail asked her grandmother, "Is Uncle Mike your son?"

Gram said, "I can't understand you with the candy in your mouth."

Abigail took the candy from her mouth, held it between her fingers, and asked again, "Is Uncle Mike your son?"

"Oh, my, no!" Gram shook her head. "Mike is your mother's brother. You remember that his name is Mike Bartlett, and your mother's name was Martha Bartlett before she married your father."

Abigail got a strange feeling that Gram was glad Uncle Mike wasn't her son. "What about Uncle George? Is he your son?"

"That's right; your father, Samuel, and your Uncle George are my sons," Gram explained. "And now it's time for you to go to bed."

"Thanks for the candy, Gram." Abigail kissed Gram good night and went on to her own room.

She looked out her bedroom window at the trees stirring in the gentle summer breeze as she got ready for bed. She could hear the low murmur of voices coming up from the study where her parents and Uncle Mike were still talking. Seemed strange on an ordinary weekday night.

As it turned out this was no ordinary weekday night and no ordinary visit, because as Gram had predicted Uncle Mike had come to stay!

Chapter Four

As Abigail opened her eyes, she had a strange feeling that something was different in the house. She sat up straight in bed, and then she remembered—Uncle Mike!

Justin got up lazily, stretched, and walked slowly to the bedroom door for Abigail to let him out. "You wait until I dress, and then I'll take you out." Justin wagged his tail as if he understood and slid down to the floor on his front paws, lying squarely in front of the door.

Abigail laughed at him, patted him on his head, and then stepped over him to run to the bathroom. Quickly she splashed water on her face, scrubbed her teeth, and came back to get into her clothes.

Justin and Abby ran downstairs together and through the kitchen. Mother called to her from the breakfast room. "Abigail, come for your breakfast," as Abigail opened the screen door and Justin bounded out.

When she turned from the kitchen into the breakfast room, she saw Uncle Mike at the breakfast table. He looked up and smiled, "Good morning, Abby."

"Hi, Uncle Mike." It really felt good to see him here but a little strange. She couldn't remember Uncle Mike ever staying overnight before.

Mother said, almost as if she were interrupting anything else that Uncle Mike and Abigail might say, "Abby, before you sit down, will you put the ice card in the window? And turn it for 50 pounds."

Abby went to the icebox and got the square card off the top. There were different numbers, 25, 50, 75, and 100, on each of the four edges, and the iceman would deliver the amount, which was at the top of the card. "Shall I put it in the window of the front porch? I think Rusty can see it better on the porch."

"That's fine," Mother replied.

"Where is everybody?" Abby asked as she sat down. It looked as if Mother had already eaten, and Uncle Mike was just finishing breakfast.

"Your father has gone to work and Caroline to school." Caroline was taking college classes in summer school. "Robert isn't down yet, and neither is your grandmother."

Abby put cornflakes into a cereal bowl, and then poured milk over them until they floated almost to the top of the bowl, and started to eat.

Mother got up from the table and went to the kitchen cabinet where she was kneading bread dough, and Uncle Mike said, "If you will excuse me, I'll clear my dishes."

He got up and took his dishes to the sink and then he got out the dishpan and soap and ran hot water into the pan.

Mother turned and looked at him, but she didn't say anything. Just then Gram walked into the kitchen and looked surprised, and Abigail thought, a little disapproving as she saw Mike doing the dishes.

Gram walked to the stove and poured a cup of coffee and then turned and said, "Good Morning…. I guess I'm a little late this morning."

Mother smiled, "Not at all. I just thought I would get a head start on the bread, since it promises to be a hot day. I will put it up to raise for the first time. And then, you can make up the loaves to raise the second time and bake it."

After breakfast Abby ran out to play with Justin, and she saw Mr. Allen sitting on his front porch across the street. Looking carefully both ways, she ran across the street, "Hi, Mr. Allen."

She loved to visit Mr. Allen…and Mrs. Allen, too…but Mr. Allen always told such interesting stories. "Hi Abby, come on up and set a spell. I haven't seen Mary Margaret yet; she must be helping her mother in the house."

Justin ran over to Mr. Allen's rocking chair and sat down waiting to be petted as Mrs. Allen came to the door. She was a pink and white, round little lady with snow-white hair piled high on her head. "Would you like a cookie, Abby?"

Mrs. Allen's cookies were always so good, but Abby was still full from breakfast. "Thanks, Mrs. A., but I just finished breakfast."

"Well, I know Justin won't turn me down." And she brought out a morsel of meat scraps and gave it to Justin, who gulped it down and looked up for more.

Mrs. Allen looked up the street, and said, "There comes Rusty with the ice truck."

Abby looked and saw that Rusty was just about four houses down, and then she saw Mary Margaret come out of her house to go down to the ice truck. "Mary Margaret," she called, "wait for me!"

The older couple laughed. "Run on, Abby, we'll see you later."

Abby and Justin caught up with Mary Margaret, and they ran down to the ice wagon. There were three or four other kids there also following the dripping ice wagon, watching Rusty as he deftly cut a line through a block of ice with his ice pick, and then with the ice tongs slung the heavy block of ice up onto the leather pad on his shoulder to carry the ice into the house.

"Can we have some ice, Rusty?" the kids were asking. He didn't seem to be paying any attention to them, but as he came back to the truck, he gave them each a sharp cold splinter of ice to suck on. When he saw Abby, he gave her an especially large piece of ice, as he asked, "Is Caroline home?"

"No, she's at school this morning," Abby answered.

Casually he turned to cut another chunk of ice and then asked again, "Does she go to school in the afternoon?"

Abby knew Caroline didn't, but she thought Caroline was probably going to be helping Morrison with his mathematics. "I'm not sure…I think she stays at school in the afternoon."

Mary Margaret and Abby went down to the corner lot where the boys were playing baseball. They stayed to watch for a while, and Abby was surprised to see Robert playing. She thought this was his morning to mow the grass. When the teams changed sides, she walked over to him and said, "I thought you had to do the grass this morning."

Robert shrugged and grinned, "I didn't have to." He looked very pleased.

When Abby went back home, she knew why Robert didn't have to cut the grass. Uncle Mike was mowing the grass! When she went into the house, Mother was in the sunroom sewing. Abby sat down on the window seat facing Mother's sewing machine. Mother looked up and said, "You got the ice sign up just in time. It was not very long after that Rusty delivered the ice."

Abby nodded, "I know. I was over at the Allen's and saw him. Mary Margaret and I went down, and he gave us some ice chips."

Mother smiled and nodded, "He always does, doesn't he?"

"Mother…" Abby started slowly.

Mother looked up from her work and said, "Yes."

"I don't understand about Uncle Mike. Is he coming for a visit?"

Mother laid her work down and turned toward Abby. The gray strands in her black hair gleamed in the sunlight. Her face was moist and pink in the summer heat, and her eyes were very clear and blue as she looked at Abby. "Uncle Mike had some misfortunes and needs a place to live, so he will be staying here with us."

"You mean forever?"

Mother shook her head, "So long as he needs a place to stay."

"Where did he sleep?" Abby asked.

"In the guestroom…he'll be staying there."

Abby didn't understand. "But he didn't bring his clothes or anything with him."

"I know," Mother answered simply.

Abby persisted, "But what happened to his car...and his clothes and...and...everything?"

"Uncle Mike does not have a job, and he couldn't pay for his car and those other things. He lost everything," Mother answered. She had a rather tight look around her mouth.

Abby did not understand. She had a vision of Uncle Mike walking down the street, losing one thing after another and not stopping to pick them up. She wanted to ask more, but her mother had picked up her sewing and was not looking at Abby anymore. She looked as if she were finished with the conversation.

Mother never did say any more about Uncle Mike's coming to live with them, but Caroline did.

Chapter Five

All the windows were open, and the hot summer breezes were blowing through the upstairs hall as Abby ran with Justin at her heels from her room to the stairs. She could see Caroline in her room as she ran past. She hesitated a moment when she saw Caroline sitting at her dressing table combing her hair. Abby pushed the door open a bit and asked whether she could come in.

"Of course, but leave Justin outside," Caroline answered as she carefully pinned her hair back just so. She then carefully powdered her face and ever so lightly patted rouge on her cheeks.

Abby went in through a narrowed opening of the door so Justin wouldn't squeeze in beside her and plopped down on the bed to watch. "Are you going out with Rusty tonight?"

"No, Morrison and I are going to a play at school."

"How come you are going with Morrison and not Rusty?" asked Abby.

Caroline laughed as she replied, "Because Morrison asked me, that's why!"

"But Rusty is always asking you, and you hardly ever go out with him!" Abby thought Rusty was so special. He was so tall and strong from lifting all the heavy ice on the ice wagon in the summer and playing football in the winter at Purdue. And, besides, he was so blond and tanned that Abby thought he looked like a Greek god. When she said that to Caroline, Caroline had just howled with laughter, "A Greek god! Spare me! "

Abby shrugged, "Well, maybe not a god…but a Greek athlete anyway."

Caroline changed the subject as she asked, "When does school start for you, Abigail?"

"Next Tuesday, the day after Labor Day." Abby found it difficult to believe that it was time for school to begin. This summer had been such fun!

"Where have you been?" Caroline looked at Abby critically, "You look so grubby!"

Abby looked down at her clothes. She was a little dirty from sitting on the ground leaning against a tree in the vacant lot. She shrugged her shoulders as she answered, "Mary Margaret and I were playing in the vacant lot."

"Oh, Abby, you know Mother doesn't like you to go there." Caroline scolded," You get all dirty, and besides who knows what goes on in the woods!"

"Oh, Caroline!" Abby exclaimed. She didn't need Caroline to tell her what to do. Caroline was such a lady! She didn't think Abby should even play catch with Robert at the vacant lot! Abby thought about Robert's baseball games. Since Uncle Mike had been at their house, Robert had not had so many chores to do. He had had more time to play baseball this summer than he ever had. Abby really was glad that Uncle Mike had come to live with them. He and Mother worked in the garden together, and Uncle Mike had helped Mother with some of the canning of fruits and vegetables. He had helped Robert pick cherries and peaches off the trees in their side yard.

Uncle Mike even helped with the dishes sometimes. Though Gram didn't seem to like that too much. But after the dishes were finished, they often played cards together, and Gram did like that.

Summer evenings were so long and pleasant. Oftentimes she and Robert would play rummy with Uncle Mike and Gram, or sometimes when Robert and Mother played chess, Father would fill in to play with the card players.

Caroline got up from the dressing table and went to the closet where she got out a pretty white dress. She slipped out of her dressing gown and slipped her dress over her head, and then smoothed her hair down. She turned toward Abby. "Is my hair all right?"

"Sure, it's fine." Caroline always looked just fine, no matter what.

Abby went back to her thoughts and said aloud, "It has been fun having Uncle Mike live with us. I hope he won't leave for a long time."

"He's not apt to," Caroline answered rather sharply.

"What do you mean?"

Caroline shrugged her shoulders, "Well, he doesn't have any money…and no job."

Abby felt like she needed to defend Uncle Mike. "I know he doesn't have a job. But how do you know he doesn't have any money?"

Caroline just looked very know-it-all as she said, "It's obvious, isn't it?"

"He had that big car; maybe he sold it and has money from that…"

"Not likely," Caroline said. "Abby, he drinks and that's why he doesn't have his car or clothes… or a job for that matter!"

"What do you mean, he drinks? What does he drink? I don't understand." Abby felt kind of creepy. She didn't know what Caroline meant, but she made Uncle Mike sound so awful.

"Oh, Abby, you just don't know about these things. He drinks liquor! He gets drunk! And that's how he lost his job, and he spent all his money getting drunk! And now he has to live with us because he has nowhere else to go!"

"How do you know? " Abby demanded.

"Because I heard Mother and Father talking about it!"

"Oh," Abby said flatly, but then she added loyally, "Well, I like having him here!"

Caroline shrugged, "It's ok, I guess. I like him, too."

Just then the grandfather clock chimed, and it had scarcely stopped when the doorbell rang. "That's probably Morrison, now. Will you get the door, Abby?"

Abby nearly fell over Justin still waiting in the hall, and she ran downstairs with Justin scrambling after her.

Morrison was standing on the front porch, looking very stiff and proper in a cream-colored suit. Abby held the door open and said, "Come on in… Caroline will be right down."

And she was. Caroline came down the stairs right behind Abby and Justin.

Gram, Uncle Mike, Robert, and Mother were playing cards at the dining room table. Uncle Mike called, "Come on, Abby, we're just starting a new game of 500 Rummy. Pull up a chair, and we'll deal you in."

"Take my place, Abby," said Mother. "I want to go in to talk to your father in the study."

Abby slipped into Mother's chair as she left the table. She looked kind of shyly at Uncle Mike. Somehow she expected him to look different... but he didn't. His eyes were just as twinkly, and his face just as crinkly as he smiled at her. He started to deal the cards. Abby liked to watch him as he skillfully shuffled the cards together and made them almost spin as they fell back into place, and then he cut the cards with a special flair, and said, as he always did, "Does anyone else want to cut?" Nobody ever did!

They had such fun playing cards. Uncle Mike didn't usually win, although he was always very close to winning and then at the last minute someone else would have a better hand and leave Uncle Mike with a handful of cards. Abby always wondered whether Uncle Mike did not do it on purpose to let the others win. The games were always exciting, and as they played cards Abby rather forgot what Caroline had said. But as they finished the game and Gram said, "Due to the lateness of the hour, I think we had better not start another game."

Abby teased, "Just one more hand, Gram... please. "

Uncle Mike collected the cards and stacked the deck on the corner of the table. "We'll be ready to play tomorrow night."

Abby's thoughts returned to Caroline saying that Uncle Mike got drunk. Abby had never seen anybody who was drunk. She studied Uncle Mike's face. She wondered how you knew. She just couldn't imagine Uncle Mike any other way than the way he was!

In spite of what Caroline had said, Abby was glad that Uncle Mike had come. His being there was the first change in the family—and for the better. He helped out, and playing cards in the evenings was always fun. But the next change was certainly not better. It was terrible!

Chapter Six

Abigail and Mary Margaret walked to school together every day. They walked single file on the big wall in front of the Allen's big old house. Justin ran along beside them, and then when they clambered down from the wall, he ran ahead of them the rest of the way until they reached the door at school. Then when they went into school, Justin ran home, but he was always there waiting for them when they got out of school.

Abigail liked school, especially Mrs. Lingle, her sixth-grade teacher. And, most especially, because Mary Margaret sat next to her. When they were supposed to be quiet, they usually did not talk to each other, but they did sometimes pass notes back and forth. Abigail was sure Mrs. Lingle knew, but she never said anything.

The weeks went past so fast. School was fun, but Abby was always glad for Saturdays and Sundays, when she could stay up late and play cards with the family, or read, or just stretch out on the floor and think.

This Saturday evening Abby felt so warm and cozy as she lay beside the open fireplace in the living room. It was the first fire of the fall in the fireplace. The air was crisp and cool outside, and she could hear the wind whistling through the trees in the side yard. The bright orange flames climbed upward in the dark fireplace. The fire crackled and snapped at the dark, shaggy logs. The large living room was dark save for the warm semi-circle of light spread by the billowing flames of the fire in the fireplace.

Abby stretched out and propped her head on her elbow to look at the eerie shadows across the ceiling. The huge mirror at the end of the living room reflected the images of Mother and Robert intent on their chess game. They each sat so still studying the chessboard. Mother's quiet face didn't reveal what she was thinking, but Robert's eyebrows were drawn together into a deep frown. At fourteen he had been playing chess for three years, but he could never be sure that he could win a game from Mother.

Uncle Mike and Gram were sitting at the dining room table playing double solitaire with only the sounds of the cards as they placed them on the table. In the study Father was working at his desk, and Caroline was curled up in an easy chair reading.

Caroline looked up from her book to ask, "Abby, did you let Justin out?"

"I sure did!" Abby replied defensively.

Smugly, Caroline said sweetly, "Then perhaps you ought to let him back in."

Abby took a deep breath. Caroline really trapped her into that. She had forgotten to let Justin back in. Abby rolled over to sit up cross-legged, and then she thought that Caroline could let the dog in just as well as she could. "Why don't you let him in, Caroline?"

"He's your dog," Caroline's answer was scornful. "You let him out; you let him in!"

Abigail couldn't think quickly of any good retort. Caroline always got the last word! She leapt to her feet and threaded her way between the chess players and Caroline's big chair. As she went into the large front hall from the living room, the air was chilly. She swung the great front door open to call for Justin, and there he stood with his tail wagging merrily.

Just then the telephone rang. And this was the phone call that changed Abby's life. "I'll get it," Abby called and ran to the dining room to answer the phone.

"Hello," Abby said as she put the receiver to her ear and spoke into the mouthpiece of the phone.

It was Uncle George, and he asked to speak to her father, so Abby said, "Just a minute, please," as she put the receiver down on the table and ran to get her father.

Caroline had put her book down and was sitting on the edge of her chair. "Is it for me?" she asked as she started to get up.

Abby shook her head. "No, it's for Father." And she ran in through to the door of the study to say, "Father, the telephone is for you."

Father got up and walked through the living room to the phone. He put his arm around Abby's shoulder as he asked her if she knew who was calling, and she told him that it was Uncle George.

"Hello, George," Father said as he answered the phone. Gram looked up from her card game, and when she heard George's name she hesitated a moment to see whether he wanted to talk to her.

After Father hung up, he said, "George and Hester are coming by tomorrow."

Mother looked up from her chess game to ask, "I hope you invited them for dinner."

Gram had gotten up from the table and walked into the living room to hear about the conversation. She nodded as Mother asked the question. She had overheard Father inviting them for Sunday dinner.

Father replied, "Yes, I did Martha. They'll be here about noon."

Abby said to herself, but everyone heard, "Oh, no!"

"What do you mean…oh, no?" Mother asked sharply.

Abby made a sour face, "Do I have to stay home with Gloria? Mary Margaret and I were going on a hike to the woods to collect leaves for school."

"What woods?" asked Mother.

Abigail shrugged her shoulders as she said softly, "In the vacant lot."

Mother looked a little cross as she answered firmly, "Abigail, you know I do not like you playing in the woods at the vacant lot."

"But we need to gather leaves for our science class!" Abigail protested.

"Then you can collect leaves in our sideyard… and up and down the street, and I am sure Gloria will be glad to go with you!" Mother replied.

Abigail nodded and thought to herself, "Sure she will!"

Father looked as if he were thinking his own thoughts, but he turned his head toward Abby and said firmly, "That is enough, Abigail."

Abby swallowed hard and looked down at Justin beside her. It was almost as if her father could read her thoughts. Father didn't usually get cross with her, and when he did, she felt awful.

Uncle George, Aunt Hester, and Gloria did come for dinner on Sunday, and they sat on one side of the dinner table with Gram sitting beside Gloria. There was something different about dinner that day. Abigail's family talked and laughed as they usually did at dinner. Uncle Mike told some funny stories, but Uncle George and Aunt Hester didn't laugh. Afterwards Abigail knew why.

After dinner Mother said, "You girls can go play after the table is cleared. Aunt Hester, Gram, and I will do the dishes, and Caroline can help."

Abigail smiled to herself as she saw Caroline's face, "Come on, Gloria, let's go outside. Let's get Mary Margaret and go to the woods." Abby gulped when she realized what she had said, but she looked at Mother who hadn't noticed. She shook her head a little as she thought to herself. Mother hadn't said that she couldn't go to the woods…only that she didn't like it!

Abigail and Gloria ran outside and down to Mary Margaret's house, who was just coming out, slipping into her heavy sweater as she ran down the steps. "Hi, Abby! Hi, Gloria!"

They turned in the path into the woods of the vacant lot. The twigs and leaves crackled under their feet as they walked. They came to the center of the woods, where there was a little clearing with a large smooth rock in the center.

Gloria sat down on the rock and looked around her as Mary Margaret and Abby scurried about gathering brightly colored leaves. They tried to get leaves from different trees. After a while they sat down, Abby on a log and Mary Margaret on the ground.

"My father may have gotten a job," Mary Margaret said as though it was something very much on her mind. "And my sister Cecilia and her husband Ralph are moving into our house with us. Ralph has a job. Mother can take care of their baby, Theresa, and maybe Cecilia can get some work." Mary Margaret said all of this almost without taking a breath, and then she smiled, "So I think everything is going to be all right."

Abby explained to Gloria that Mary Margaret almost had to move because her father lost his job.

Gloria looked a little strange, as if she were going to say something. And then she didn't. She lifted her head up and looked away as if she were just very snooty and not interested.

Gloria hopped down from the rock. "Let's go back now."

When they got back home, Abby understood why Gloria had looked strange. Uncle George also had lost his job, but he had not been able to find another, so Uncle George, Aunt Hester, and Gloria were going to move in with them!

Chapter Seven

Everything changed when Gloria came! Aunt Hester and Uncle George moved into Uncle Mike's room…that is, the guestroom where Uncle Mike had been staying, and Uncle Mike moved to the attic.

It didn't seem right to Abby that Uncle Mike had to go to the attic. It was cold and dark up there. And, besides, he was here first! Mike packed up his few belongings, and in no time the guestroom was cleaned and ready for Aunt Hester to move their things in.

That was only the beginning; Abigail knew that the house was going to be overcrowded when Gloria moved in, but little did she know that not only was she going to have to live in the same house with that creep, but to even share her room! Abby asked hopefully, "Will Gloria be sharing the room with her parents?"

Mother looked Abigail squarely in the eye, as if to say, Abigail, you know that is ridiculous, and then after a moment's pause, said in her firm, no-nonsense voice, "No, Abigail, you and Gloria will be sharing your room."

Only to herself, she couldn't say it out loud, Abigail groaned, "Oh no!" It wasn't that Gloria was terrible, it was only that she was always right! And so superior about being right! And she had to have her own way all the time!

And that started right off. "I'll take the bed by the window," Gloria announced as she brought in a load of clothes, books, and toys and dumped them on the bed.

"But I sleep in that bed," Abigail protested. At night she loved to lie in bed and look out the window at the tree branches swaying in the side yard. Thinking maybe she could change Gloria's mind, slyly she said, "The other twin bed is easier to make because you can get all around it. And that one is really hard because you can't get around it on the window side."

But it didn't work! Gloria answered sweetly, "How nice…then that will be easier for you, won't it?"

And that was only the beginning! Gloria's clothes had to be fit into the closet…her books on the shelves…Abigail had to move her stack of movie magazines and her rock collection. But the final insult came when Aunt Hester said that Justin had to go!

Well, it wasn't exactly Aunt Hester. Really, it was Mother, but only after Aunt Hester said that because Gloria had asthma she couldn't sleep in the same room with a dog, much less a big, furry dog like Justin.

"Everything is changing just everything!" Abigail cried as she burst into tears. "I have to have Gloria in my room, and now I can't even have Justin! He always sleeps right by my bed!"

Mother had that tight-lipped look that she got when she was just next to losing her temper. "I know, so close by your bed that you fall over him every time you get out of bed!"

Abigail flounced out of the room as she couldn't keep from crying. Mother took a deep breath and went to Abby and took her in her arms. She dried Abby's tears with her apron, and she sighed deeply, and her voice tone changed as she said, "Abby, I know that it isn't easy for you to share your room with Gloria. It isn't easy for any of us, but stop and think of their family. It isn't easy for them either to have to move in with us. Remember Gloria has always had her own room, too, and it isn't her choice to have to come here. Not only did she have to move out of her own home; Gloria is going to have to change schools as well."

Abigail drew back. She hadn't even thought of that, "Oh, no! She won't be in my room at school will she?"

Mother took a deep breath as she answered in a very matter-of-fact tone. "I don't know. We will just have to see. You can take her to school with you on Monday."

Abigail gasped as she thought about Gloria going to school with her. Then her thoughts turned back to her indignation about Justin. "Mother! Where is Justin supposed to sleep?"

"Oh, probably where he should have been sleeping all along…in the play house. That makes a good doghouse," Mother answered.

"Oh, no!" Abby wailed. "It's too cold out there. He'll freeze!"

"Nonsense. He has a good, heavy fur coat. He'll be just fine."

Abby didn't believe that for a minute. She knew he would be cold and unhappy, and he would probably bark all night!

Mother told her to get an old blanket from the basement to make a bed for Justin, and to take him out there so he could know that it was for him.

Grudgingly, Abigail dragged the blanket along behind her and walked with Justin out the back walk. Justin bounded along happily, with his plume of a tail wagging merrily. It made Abigail sad to look at him. He didn't know that he was going to be put out in the cold.

As she opened the door of the playhouse, she was startled to see a shadow of someone sitting on the back corner by the stairs, and then she smelt the aroma of a pipe, and she knew it was Uncle Mike.

"What are you doing out here?" Abby asked.

"It's a good place to smoke my pipe," Uncle Mike answered calmly. "Come on in. What are you doing with that big blanket?"

Abby didn't answer, but instead asked, "Why are you smoking out here? You usually smoke your pipe while you're playing cards."

"Well," Uncle Mike answered easily, "Smoke bothers Hester, and I thought it better not to smoke in the house."

Abigail dropped the blanket from her arms, set her mouth firmly, and crossed her arms across her chest. "Boy, it seems like everything changed when THEY moved in, and they haven't even been here a whole day yet! You had to move to the bed in the attic, and it's cold up there and dark…and it isn't fair…and Gloria moved into my room with me…and now Justin has to sleep outside!" Abby set her mouth. She just did not understand. Her whole world was changing, and there was nothing she could do about it.

Uncle Mike shook his head and smiled wryly, "Don't get all worked up into a tizzy, Abby. Everything is going to be all right. I don't mind sleeping on the third floor. There is plenty of space. I like sleeping in a cool room, and there is a fine light bulb in the ceiling, which I can turn on to read in bed. I don't spend that much time in my room anyway. I only go there to sleep. Besides, don't forget, your folks are very good to me to let me stay here…and I'll only be here until I get a job."

"It just doesn't seem right…you were here first!"

"Well, maybe that's just the reason, that I need to get a job and move along, and your folks can help out George and his family until they can get work and some money." Uncle Mike's brown eyes looked soft and crinkled as he smiled at Abby, "It won't be forever."

Abby felt a little better about Uncle Mike. He didn't seem to mind, but then she felt her anger rise again. As she said, "Justin is going to have to sleep outside in the playhouse. Because Glor-i-a can't have him sleeping in our room. Aunt Hester says he will make Gloria sneeze."

"Oh, well, if that's the case…that is just the way it is. I don't think Justin will mind too much, will you, old boy?" Mike reached over and rubbed Justin on the head. Justin cuddled up to Mike and turned over to have his chest rubbed, too.

"I think I'll go get Mary Margaret."

Uncle Mike puffed on his pipe, and the smoke rolled around his head. He nodded, "You need to tell her what's going on?"

"Uh-huh," Abigail ran around the corner of the house. She felt a good kind of closeness to Uncle Mike. He seemed to understand what she was thinking a lot of the time.

Chapter Eight

Abigail ran around the house to the front walk, just in time to see Mary Margaret skipping down the street. When she caught up, they walked along together. Abigail talked as fast as she could as she told Mary Margaret all the problems with Gloria. And Mary Margaret just listened at first, and then she asked questions as she agreed with Abby about how awful it must be. As they walked and talked Abby happened to glance up at her bedroom window and saw Gloria looking out at them. Gloria's face looked very serious, and perhaps a little sad. Abigail felt a small unpleasant feeling of guilt deep inside. She almost felt sorry for Gloria, but she shook the feeling because she would rather be mad at her!

Mary Margaret thought about Gloria as Abby was talking. She really didn't like Gloria very well either, but she felt she had to say, "I bet

Gloria didn't want to move from her own house."
She remembered how awful she felt when she
thought she was going to have to move.

Abby felt like she needed to change the
subject. She started to run, "Come on, let's go
over to the Allen's."

Mr. and Mrs. Allen were grandparent kind of
people. Mr. Allen didn't work anymore, that is, at
a job. He loved to work in their garden, and Mrs.
Allen loved to cook. They both were so nice to all
the kids in the neighborhood. Mr. Allen loved to
tell stories about the olden days, and Mrs. Allen
always seemed to enjoy listening.

Mr. Allen flung open the door before they had
even rung the bell. He had seen the girls coming
up the walk, and he was always glad when they
came to visit.

"Abby, Mary Margaret,…what's going on?"
He asked cheerfully. "Come on in. Mother
has just made some sweet rolls, and she needs
someone to taste them."

Mr. Allen always called Mrs. Allen, Mother,
although obviously she was not his mother, and
she always called him Mr. Allen. Just then she
came bustling out of the kitchen. Her pink face
was just a little pinker from her baking. "Girls,
you are just in time to taste the first panful from
the oven. Sit down, and I'll bring them in."

The air was filled with the lovely smell of
baking cinnamon rolls. Their house always

smelled so good with the delicious smells from Mrs. Allen's kitchen.

Mary Margaret sat primly on one of the rocking chairs, and Abby sat on the floor by Mr. Allen's chair.

Did I ever tell you the story about when I was a boy in Kansas and we used to play baseball with the Indians? The Haskell Indian Nations University had a championship baseball team, and I played with the Lawrence Boys Baseball Team…"

"Mr. Allen, I think you did tell the girls about that," Mrs. Allen said as she handed each of the girls a plate with a hot cinnamon bun. Then she asked with interest, "What's going on at your house, Abigail? Do you have visitors?"

Abigail kind of screwed up her face as she thought that she wished it was just visitors! And, then she answered, "Well, yes, or, really, I guess they are moving in for keeps." And then she told about Gloria and her mother and father moving in because Uncle George lost his job.

Mrs. Allen wagged her head, "That's happening more and more…how lucky that you have a good big house. Your Uncle Mike is there, too, isn't he?"

Abigail had that vision in her head again of everybody cramming in the house, and the whole house blowing up like a big balloon, because it was so full of people! Then she saw Mrs. Allen looking at her with interest as she waited for her answer.

Abby counted, "There's our family, Mother, Father, Caroline, Robert and Gram and me... that's six...and Uncle Mike and now three more...that makes ten...and Justin, but he has to sleep outside now."

"How's that?" Mr. Allen asked.

"Oh, Gloria...." She hesitated a bit and then went on, "Gloria doesn't like dogs, and she is sharing my room with me, so Justin has to sleep in the playhouse."

"Doesn't like dogs?" Mr. Allen asked in disbelief.

And Abby felt a little guilty again and corrected what she had said, "Well, really it isn't that she doesn't like Justin.... She is allergic to dogs."

Mr. Allen nodded as he said, "Oh, I see. And how old is Gloria?"

"She's my age. She'll be 12 in May."

"Oh, so she will be going to school with you. Will she be in your room at school?"

"I hope not!" Then Abby again felt a little bad at sounding so mean. "There are two sixth-grade rooms, so maybe she'll be in Miss Johnson's room."

Mr. Allen looked a little thoughtful and as if he weren't quite listening. "I think Mother and I are going to move across town with SaraLou and her family." SaraLou was the Allen's daughter.

Mrs. Allen smiled a very weak smile, and added, "Just for the winter. We think we may be able to rent this house, which will help us out a little with money. Then it just makes sense not to spend the money to heat two houses, and we can help SaraLou out with the children."

"Oh, no! You can't move out of the neighborhood!" Abigail exclaimed. She just couldn't imagine the neighborhood without the Allens.

"We'll be back," Mr. Allen reassured Abby, "when money is a little easier."

Abigail and Mary Margaret talked about it later. They didn't understand what Mr. Allen meant when he had said, "when money is a little easier."

On Monday, Mary Margaret and Abigail walked to school, but Justin didn't go with them, and they didn't walk the Allens' wall. They walked with Gloria and her mother to school. Gloria and Aunt Hester went into the principal's office, and Abby and Mary Margaret went on into their schoolroom. Abigail kept watching the clock. It ticked away slowly as Mrs. Lingle started the school day with the Pledge of Allegiance, and then they started to work on their social studies projects.

When the clock reached nine o'clock, Mary Margaret passed a note to Abby that said, "She probably is going to be in Miss Johnson's room, isn't she?"

Abby read the note and quickly wrote back, "I hope so!"

And then the door opened and in walked Aunt Hester and Gloria.

Chapter Nine

Abigail decided after a while that it wasn't just awful having Gloria at their house. It seemed strange to have her in the same room at school, and Gloria did tell her mother everything that happened, but sometimes it wasn't so bad. Gloria could run fast, and Abigail's friends always picked Gloria to be on their teams when they played games at recess or in gym, and that was kind of neat. However, it was a little embarrassing when Gloria always got the best grade in the class on anything they did.

The warm, golden days of autumn seemed to go by so fast. Abby and Mary Margaret almost always invited Gloria to go with them to play. Sometimes, though, they would go to the woods just to be by themselves to read and talk.

At night it seemed cozy to have such a large family, and the house didn't seem so stretched out like a balloon. Abby felt like the house had settled in to being just right for the people in it. Gloria sat at the side table in the dining room doing her homework, while Abby usually stretched out on the living room floor. When Caroline was home, she often sat at the dining room table working on her papers and schoolwork while Uncle Mike and Gram played cards at the other end of the dining room table. Father more often than not worked in the study. But this night in early November, he and Uncle George, Mother, and Aunt Hester were sitting in the living room around the fireplace talking, and Robert was playing rummy with Gram and Uncle Mike.

Abigail was writing a story for language arts, and she frowned as she thought about what she wanted to write. Her story was really about Justin. She felt so sad that he had to be outside in the cold. She wrote quickly as she imagined her story about a dog whose family moved away and left him…and his adventures in trying to find his family again.

Mother interrupted Abby's thoughts when she asked, "Abby, how can you write like that? You haven't enough light, and I don't know how you can write half lying-down."

Without stopping her writing, Abby scrambled to sit up against the door jam between the living room and dining room and went on with her story.

The conversation of the grownups was in the background. They were talking about the presidential election as they did almost every evening.

Abby remembered this particular conversation well because it was the night that Father told them that their telephone would be taken out.

Mother was saying, almost defiantly for her, "I have considered all the issues, and I have made up my mind to vote for Franklin Delano Roosevelt. With the sad affairs of the country, I think it is time to make a change. President Hoover is getting no place in solving our problems."

Aunt Hester shook her head, "I have always voted Republican, but with no jobs, no money... Something has to change!"

"I believe President Hoover is making progress," Father said with conviction. "I think we should give him the opportunity to put things right. The job and the money situation simply have to improve!"

"Samuel, I have to disagree with you," Uncle George got to his feet and went over to stand by the fireplace. "There is no reason to believe that things are getting better or are ever going to get better. As you know, I have been job hunting every day, with no success, and it seems to me that it is growing worse, not better!"

Caroline stopped her work and turned her chair around to listen. "Morrison Strawn's father said that he is going to vote for Herbert Hoover."

"Woop-te-do! That makes it right!" Abigail taunted.

Mother frowned, "Abigail, please make your comments only when they add to the conversation."

Although Uncle George smiled, the corners of his lips turned down instead of up when he said, "I talked to Mr. Strawn about a job, and his business is very bad and getting worse every day under the Hoover administration."

Caroline shrugged. She hadn't known that Uncle George had talked to Mr. Strawn about a job. She did know that Uncle George dressed every morning as if he were going to business. He left at the regular time and didn't return until evening, spending all day every day trying to find a job.

Caroline turned and asked Uncle Mike, "What do you think?"

Abby gave Caroline a dirty look. She thought Caroline was being far too fresh. She knew Caroline was just trying to embarrass Uncle Mike!

Caroline paid no attention to Abby's dirty look. She wanted to push Uncle Mike into an answer. She felt that he was far too casual in looking for work. Uncle Mike helped with the morning work, dishes, gardening, and odd jobs around the house, and then some days he would go out to look for work.

Mike looked up from his hand of cards, deliberately made a discard and then answered, "I haven't decided yet whether I'll vote for Hoover or Roosevelt."

Caroline pushed a little more as she pointedly asked Uncle Mike, "Do you think there are any jobs?"

Unruffled, Mike said, "Yes, I think there are some, but not very many…and lots of people for every job that's open." He knew Caroline was pushing him.

Abigail put her writing pad beside her and stood up. She was so annoyed at Caroline, but she couldn't think of anything to say. Caroline was just being mean…trying to make Uncle Mike look bad.

"Well, if we were to vote tonight, it looks like Hester, George, and I would vote for Roosevelt. Mike is undecided and only you for Hoover, Samuel," said Mother.

Gram interrupted vigorously, "Martha, you didn't count my vote! I have voted Republican ever since women had the vote, and the men in our family have always voted Republican. I am not about to change! I will vote for Hoover!"

Mother smiled with a little embarrassment.

"Well, I guess our family vote is: three for Roosevelt, two for Hoover, and one undecided."

Abigail remembered that evening conversation later at the Sunday dinner when the family had no money because President Roosevelt had closed the banks. And so did Gram!

Father changed the subject with a real bombshell, which really got Caroline's attention! "Martha, the telephone company will be out tomorrow to take out the phone. Everyone needs to know that after tomorrow we will not be receiving phone calls. If you absolutely need to make a call, it will be necessary to use the pay phone at Ford's Grocery Store at the corner."

Caroline leaped to her feet and faced her father, "I don't understand. What do you mean? Do you mean we won't have a phone at all!"

Abigail didn't understand either, and Robert looked kind of blank.

Father answered calmly, "I am sorry that this is necessary, but we simply cannot afford the telephone bill. We need to use our money in the most important ways…for food, the house, heat, and what few clothes we have to buy."

Uncle George's face grew red, and he almost stammered as he said, "I'll be getting a job soon… and then we can help out."

"George, this is not your fault," Father said hastily. "We would have had the phone taken out whether or not you had been here. It is simply a luxury we can do without."

"Luxury!" wailed Caroline. "How can I talk to my friends? I'll never have another date! No one will be able to call me!"

Mother raised her chin and took a deep breath. "Caroline, we all need to make changes. I am truly sorry, but I am sure your boyfriends will find ways to get in touch with you."

"I will give you the money I make tutoring and that can go toward the phone bill," Caroline pleaded.

Father shook his head, "No, you need that money for your school expenses at Madame Baker's. And, it is very important that you finish college so that you can teach."

"And there probably won't be any teaching jobs when I get out of school...the way things are going!" Caroline cried petulantly and then she ran upstairs. Abby could see that she was crying.

Chapter Ten

Abby was puzzled. A house without a telephone! Her imagination again saw that house with all its bulging sides, packed with people, and now it was as if it was floating with no connection to anyone else. How would they call to talk to anyone?

How could you have a house without a telephone? She had never thought about a telephone costing money. Slowly Abigail went up the stairs as all these thoughts were tumbling about in her head. At the top of the stairs, she stopped and turned into Gram's room. Only Gloria was already there, just like she belonged there! Abby felt a swell of resentment coming up in her throat. Gloria was an intruder! Every night Abby always stopped to visit with Gram before she went to bed. Just the two of them. Then her eyebrows wrinkled together as she was overcome with a frown. An unwelcome thought came into her mind. As unpleasant as it seemed, she knew that Gloria was Gram's granddaughter, too. It didn't seem right, but her head told her it was true. Right or wrong, it just wasn't the same with Gloria there!

Gram looked just the same, and maybe even pleased to have both Gloria and Abby there. Though she wasn't smiling, she looked very pleasant and calm. She reached for her crystal candy dish and offered each girl a peppermint drop. She sat rocking in her chair as she waited for the girls to talk.

Abby felt sad that Caroline was so unhappy. Caroline always seemed to have everything just the way she wanted it. And she never cried! But Abby really didn't want to say anything about Caroline in front of Gloria.

"Gram, is it just terrible not to have a phone?" Abby asked, thinking of Caroline.

Gram leaned her head back as she rocked back and forth. "Abby, I lived many years without a telephone and did just fine! When your fathers were little boys, we lived in the country miles from the nearest neighbors and didn't have a phone. When we needed something, or to ask for help, your grandfather would have to hitch up a horse and go to get it. My goodness, here we have neighbors so close we could almost shout out the window and someone would answer us."

"But how will Caroline's friends call her?" Abby asked.

"They can talk when they see one another and make plans then for their social arrangements."

"It really isn't all that bad…then is it?" Abby asked Gram for reassurance.

"No, of course not. Your father has to work out the money the best he can, and he thinks this is the best way. I am sure it won't be for too long, anyway."

Gloria sucked on her peppermint and didn't say anything. Her large brown eyes were shiny in the lamplight. Abby wondered what she was thinking, and she soon knew when Gloria said softly, almost as if she didn't want to say it, but had to, "You don't think it's because we came, do you?"

Abby was shocked; she didn't think Gloria even cared about anyone but herself!

Gram got up from her chair and put her arm around Gloria, "No, of course not. You heard your Uncle Samuel say that had nothing to do with it." Abby felt a little twinge of guilt about feeling so mean about Gloria, and it was hard for her to share Gram with her. Then Gram put her other arm around Abby and patted them both, "It's time for the two of you to go to bed."

So the phone was taken out, leaving a gaping hole in the wall where the box had been. Caroline didn't say much, but when she needed to make a phone call, she would announce loudly, "I am going down to the corner to use the pay phone." And there were certainly more callers at the door asking to talk with Caroline.

Then the Allens moved. It seemed so strange, really odd, when they moved most of their furniture out. Abigail and Mary Margaret sat on their front wall and watched sadly as SaraLou's husband and Mr. Allen carried out the chairs and the sideboard from the dining room. Abby's father and Uncle George went over to help. No one talked much as they moved the furniture. At last Mrs. Allen came out, wrapped up in her winter coat and a scarf tied over her head. She looked so little, and her face was so serious, not at all like her rosy, round self.

Abby walked over to her slowly and said, "Bye, Mrs. Allen."

Mrs. Allen smiled wanly, "We'll be back. We'll be back soon…probably next summer."

Mr. Allen came and hugged Abby and Mary Margaret. "You both do well in school this winter, so next summer you can tell me what you have learned." Then he turned to his wife and said, "Come on, Mother." And they climbed into the truck with SaraLou's husband.

Abby felt the hot tears rise in her eyes, and she had such a lump in her throat. Somehow it seemed as if they would never be back, and it would never be the same again!

She ran home with Mary Margaret running behind her. She heard her father say to Uncle George, "I sure hate to see them leave."

Robert was explaining to Mother as they were walking back home. He had just gotten a paper route, and he was so excited! "I'll have 40 customers where I'll deliver *The Indianapolis Star* each morning."

"Where will you pick up the papers?" Mother asked.

"At the corner of 42nd street; then I can go right on to deliver them."

Father heard what they were saying and asked, "Where is your route?"

"On Washington Boulevard, Pennsylvania, and Meridian Streets between 42nd and 46th streets...to all those big homes."

"That sounds good, but what about your school work? Will you be able to get up that early, go to school, and still have time to do your homework?" Father asked.

"Sure, there'll be no problem," Robert was ecstatic. "But just think of the money I'll make. I'll really be able to help out!"

"I'll help, too," Abby volunteered eagerly.

And she did. Sometimes Gloria went, too. It was kind of exciting to get up so early and go down to the corner in the cold, dark morning. They took a stack of papers, crouched down to roll each one into a neat roll and fasten the top paper into the slot, just so. Then they stuffed the papers into the big cloth bag, which Robert hung on the back of his bike, or sometimes, they took the red wagon and put the papers in there, and he pulled the wagon. As they went down the street, Robert would call out the addresses and Abby would run on and throw the paper on the front stoop of each house. After a while, she got so she knew all the houses, too. When the route was finished, they walked home together. The darkness would be melting away as the rays of the rising sun floated over the houses from the east. And the whole world just felt so good!

Mother was waiting for them with steaming cups of hot chocolate on the kitchen table, when they came in the kitchen door. They sat and talked, just the three of them…and even when Gloria went it was fun, although Abby liked it best when she didn't.

When Election Day came and all the grown ups in the family went to the polls in the basement of the church, the votes of the Graham family had changed from Mother's count to an unanimous vote of the family for Franklin Delano Roosevelt!

Uncle Mike announced the night before that after much consideration, he felt that the country had to have a change and, therefore, he was going to cast his ballot for Roosevelt. Father was very serious as he agreed with Mike. "I have come to the same conclusion. I, too, am going to have to vote for Roosevelt."

Gram looked very serious. Her lips were pursed as though she was going to speak but she said nothing. On the next day when she went to the polls with Father and George, she still was very quiet. When she came out of the voting booth she was very pale. She did not say a word until she got home. Mother looked at her with a questioning look, but neither woman said anything.

Abby was so curious. After all the family talks about the election…and now everyone had voted for Roosevelt except maybe Gram.

"Gram," Abby blurted out, "did you vote for Hoover?"

Mother frowned and scolded, "We each have the right to the secrecy of our own vote, Abby."

"That's all right. She has the right to ask." Gram took a deep breath and then answered quietly, "I voted for Roosevelt. For the first time in my life, I voted for a Democrat. I certainly hope it was the right thing to do!" Then she said briskly, "Now it is time to start dinner!" And with that, she marched out to the kitchen, put on her apron, and started to peel potatoes.

Chapter Eleven

Thanksgiving dinner was the same festive celebration it was every year. Dinner was a feast! The delectable, honey brown roasted turkey rested on its silver platter before Father. Mother and Gram and even Aunt Hester had cooked for days preparing noodles, dressing, candied yams, cranberry sauce, home-baked dinner rolls, and Gram had made her yummy persimmon pudding.

It seemed so right to have the entire family around the dinner table. The candlelight was warm and glowing over the festive table, laden with all the good food and gleaming with Mother's sparkling crystal and shining silver. They always had the entire family for Thanksgiving dinner, only it used to be that all the guests went home after dinner.

After dinner, the table was cleared, and the pies and desserts were placed on the sideboard for evening snacks. All of the women went to the kitchen to do the dishes just as quickly as they could to get on with the pleasures of the afternoon. Mother assigned the tasks. "Caroline, you wash…"

Caroline protested, "I'll ruin my nails."

Mother paid no attention, "Gram and I will put the leftovers away. Hester, would you put the dishes away after Abigail and Gloria dry?"

Uncle Mike was the only one of the men who came into the kitchen, and he rolled up his sleeves and took over the dishwashing from Caroline, so she could help with the drying. He washed much faster than Caroline had, and soon they were all done.

After dinner, Father set up a card table in front of the fireplace, and Mother, Father, Aunt Hester, and Uncle George played euchre, a card game, which they always enjoyed.

"Uncle Mike, will you play rummy with me?" Abigail asked.

"Sure, but we need two more," Uncle Mike answered.

Gram answered quickly, "I'll take a hand. Come on, Gloria, let's sit at the side table in the dining room."

They had just gotten the game underway, when Morrison came to the door. Robert answered the door and said, "Oh, good, come on in. How would you like to play ping-pong?"

Caroline came up behind Robert and gave him a sideways glance, but they all went to the basement to play ping-pong. After a short while, Robert called up, "Any one else for ping-pong?"

The rummy game had come to the end of a hand with Gram laying down her spreads of cards and going out. She said, "Oh, I think I'd like to take a little nap. Why don't you all go on down and play ping-pong?"

At which, Mike said, "I think I would like to smoke my pipe. I'll just step outside. You two girls go on down and play."

That was about six o' clock. Gloria and Abigail played doubles with Morrison and Robert while Caroline watched. Then they played the winners with Robert slamming the ping-pong balls so hard, Abby couldn't even see them when they came to her end of the table. They all laughed and laughed as they tried to find the balls as they went off the table and bounced around on the floor. Finally Morrison quit playing and went over to sit by Caroline.

Robert laid his paddle down as he announced, "I'm getting hungry. I think I'll go up and have a piece of pie."

"Hungry? How could anyone be hungry after eating so much at dinner?" Gloria exclaimed.

"Ok, then do you want to play?" Abby asked Caroline and Morrison, who were talking softly to each other. They didn't answer. So she said a little louder, "Do the two of you want to play doubles against Gloria and me?"

"I don't think so, Abby," Caroline answered.

"So do you want to play another game, Gloria?"

Gloria shrugged, "I think I'll go upstairs."

"Ok, then…" Abby didn't care. She didn't really want to play with Gloria anyway. She thought that maybe Gram and Uncle Mike would be ready to play cards again. But they weren't. And that is how she happened to go out on the front porch.

Abby ran upstairs and looked for Uncle Mike at the table where he often played solitaire, and when he wasn't there, she looked around the living room. Then she asked of no one in particular, "Where is Uncle Mike?"

"Not here…maybe he went up to his room," Father answered as he looked up from his card game.

Abby ran up the stairs and went to the bottom of the stairs to the third floor and called up tentatively, "Uncle Mike!" She didn't want to wake him if he were taking a nap, although she didn't remember his ever taking a nap in the afternoon. She listened, but there was no answer.

She thought that maybe he was still outside smoking his pipe, but it was awfully cold. She grabbed her jacket from her room and quickly slipped into it and ran out the front door. The cold air felt good. The evening was soft and dark, and the white fluffy snow was floating down. Uncle Mike wasn't on the porch. She looked up and down the street, but there was no one out. The snow swirled around in myriads of patterns in the golden light of the streetlight on the corner. Abby shivered a little as she wondered where Uncle Mike could be in the cold.

As she looked around the neighborhood, she noticed a flickering light in the Allen's house. She watched it for a moment. The house went dark, and then she saw it again. She was puzzled. She didn't think that the Allens were there.

As she went back into the house, her mother called, "Abigail, what are you doing?"

Abby ran into the living room, and her mother chided, "Abby, you are dripping on the rug! What were you doing outside?"

"I was looking for Uncle Mike, and he wasn't outside, but I thought I saw a light in the Allen's house."

Aunt Hester looked up from her cards and said casually, "Perhaps, the Allens are there."

Mother frowned as she replied, "Oh, I don't think they would be over there now! Samuel, perhaps you ought to go see."

Father laid his cards on the table, "Abby, are you sure the light wasn't just a reflection from the street light?"

"No. I'm sure there was a light inside; it was very dim."

Father got up from the card table, walked over to the hall tree to get his heavy wool scarf, which he wrapped around his neck, and went out the front door onto the porch. Abby ran along with him. As they looked through the falling snow, the Allen's house looked dark and empty. "Watch." Abby said as she pointed toward the upper window. They waited and watched, but there was nothing to see but dark, empty windows.

Father put his arm around Abby's shoulder and said, "Let's go back in. I don't see anything now; we'll go over tomorrow to see about it."

Just then a dark figure came around the corner of the house. Father pushed Abby behind him and called, "Who is there?" And when he recognized that it was Mike, he called to him, "Where have you been?"

Abby peered out around her father and looked at Uncle Mike, who looked a little different. He seemed to be a little unsteady on his legs. He slipped and almost fell as he came up the porch steps.

Father gave Abby a little nudge and said curtly, "Go on into the house, Abigail."

Abby went in, but through the open door she could hear her father talking to Mike, and his voice sounded cross. Then she heard her father say, "Go on up to your room, Mike."

Out of the corner of her eye as she ran to hang up her coat she saw Uncle Mike go through the hallway and up the stairs.

Father looked very serious as he walked back into the house. He unwrapped his scarf from around his neck and hung it up on the hall tree.

Mother had gotten up from the card table and came to the doorway. "What was it, Samuel?" she asked anxiously.

"We couldn't see anything at the Allen's house tonight. It looked to be dark, but we will go over in the morning to see." Then he lowered his voice, "but we need to talk about Mike."

Chapter Twelve

Abby could hardly wait for Christmas vacation, and the weeks between Thanksgiving and Christmas went by so slowly.

The next day after Thanksgiving, Father and Uncle George went over to the Allen's house to see whether there was anything amiss. They found the back door standing open, so they went in and looked around. The Allens had taken most of the furniture, but it did look as if someone had been in the house.

Father went down to the corner grocery store to use the telephone to call Mr. Allen at his daughter's house. Later in the day, SaraLou and her husband brought Mr. Allen over to check the house. It was clear that someone had been in the house. It looked as if someone had slept there and perhaps had taken a few things, but it was hard to tell just what.

Mr. Allen locked up the house again and shook his head. "I can't imagine why anyone would want to get in; we didn't leave that much in the house," and he thanked Father for letting them know.

Father said that he would watch and if he saw anything more, he would call the police.

"If you hear of anyone who needs a place to live, we would like to have someone rent it," Mr. Allen said.

Uncle George spoke up quickly, "We'd sure like to rent your house. Just as soon as I can locate work, I'll be in touch with you."

Uncle George repeated his conversation with Mr. Allen to Aunt Hester when he came back into the house. She took a deep breath and said, "I would like that very much."

Abigail didn't say anything. She just looked down at Justin on her lap and thought to herself that she would like that very much, too!

Other than that excitement at the Allen's house, nothing seemed to change; however, there was a different feeling in the family. Uncle Mike hardly ever played cards with them in the long winter evenings, and he didn't talk much. He usually helped with the dinner dishes, although Gram acted as if he didn't belong in the kitchen. Then shortly after the dishes were done, he went up to his room on the third floor.

One night as Abigail was going to sleep, she kept thinking about how cold it must be up on the third floor. She said, "I wonder why Uncle Mike goes up to his room instead of staying down to play cards with us like he used to."

Gloria raised up on her elbow in her bed and said smugly, "It's because everyone is mad at him."

Abigail set her mouth. She was sorry she had said anything to Gloria, who always knew everything!

"My mother says that your father told him that the next time he comes home drunk, he has to leave."

"What do you mean?" exclaimed Abigail.

"Oh Abby, you know that he got drunk Thanksgiving night!"

Abigail turned over and pulled the covers over her head. She didn't want to hear anymore. Gloria always knew it all! But she thought back to Thanksgiving evening, when she had gone out on the porch to find Uncle Mike…and then much later he had come around the corner of the house. She remembered her father sending her inside while he talked with Uncle Mike. And then she remembered how Uncle Mike had walked kind of funny as he went on upstairs. She had such a dismal feeling in her chest, and tears rolled down her cheeks. She didn't quite know why she was crying, but she felt just terrible!

Abigail didn't want to talk to Gloria anymore. She just didn't want to hear what Gloria had to say…Gloria was always such a know-it-all!

Abigail tried not to talk to Gloria, and for a week or so she didn't. Then as Christmas time drew near, Abigail got swept up with the Christmas spirit, and she kind of forgot to be mad at Gloria. There were so many preparations for the holidays. At school they were practicing Christmas music for the Christmas program, which was on Thursday night before the last day of school before Christmas vacation. Mother and Father, Uncle George, Aunt Hester, and Gram all came, and they said it was the best Christmas program they had ever heard!

On Friday, Gloria, Mary Margaret, and Abigail walked home together, each carrying the presents they had made at school for their parents. Mrs. Lingle had brought white tissue paper and some red cord for them to wrap the presents to take home.

Gloria had woven placemats for her mother and father. Mary Margaret and Abigail had each made ceramic bowls. Abigail had loved shaping the clay with that gooky, sloppy feeling as she smoothed the rounded bowl. It had to dry for several days, and then she painted it a gorgeous purple and trimmed it with a golden yellow. After that dried, she painted it with a clear coating, which made it shiny.

After school was out, the time went quickly. Abigail, Gloria, and Gram baked Christmas cookies. They rolled them out, and then with their cookie cutters, made Santa Clauses, Christmas trees, stars, rocking horses, and gingerbread men and little dogs. Then they decorated them with all different colors of sugar and frosting. The kitchen smelled so good! When all the kitchen tables and counters and the dining room table were covered with plates of cooling cookies, all of the members of the family came through to admire and sample.

The next day, they put the cookies on plates, wrapped them in white tissue paper and placed a sprig of holly on top of each plate. Under Gram's direction, Gloria and Abby made up ten plates. Then they delivered them: first one to Mrs. Lingle's house, and one to the pastor, and one to Mary Margaret's family. Father drove them across town to take one to the Allens. There was one for the milkman, and the mailman, and one for Caroline to take to Morrison Strawn's parents. And then they took a plate of cookies to each of their neighbors on their block.

Christmas Eve all of the family, except Uncle Mike, went to the candlelight service at the church. The Christmas tree in the corner of the church sanctuary glistened with the silver icicles swaying back and forth with the slight movement of the warm air. The soft lights in the darkened church gave Abigail such a special feeling. Their family took up a whole pew. There were Father and Mother, Caroline, Robert, Abigail, and Gram. Next to Gram were Uncle George, Aunt Hester, and Gloria.

At the end of the service, the congregation all filed out of the nearly darkened church into the night where the bright starlight was reflecting on the soft white snow. They walked along together, soundlessly with only the crunch of the snow underfoot. There seemed to be a bond of silence, with each of them thinking their own thoughts on this crisp, sparkling Christmas Eve.

Christmas morning held its eternal wonder. The Christmas tree was ablaze with its colored lights; the fire in the fireplace was blazing brightly; and on every table, shelf, and mantle were candles glowing and flickering with their golden light.

Aunt Hester had made dresses for Abigail and Gloria, and they were beautiful. Abby's was red percale with little blue flowers, and Gloria's was blue with little pink flowers, made exactly alike with large white linen collars.

There were gifts under the tree for everyone; most of the gifts were handmade. There were knitted sweaters, mufflers, mittens, and gloves. There were playing cards and ping-pong balls and a Chinese checkers game for everyone to share. Something for everyone!

But after all the gifts had been opened, there were still two gifts not yet unwrapped under the tree for Uncle Mike who was not there.

Abigail wondered, but no one seemed even to notice that he was missing. It wasn't until Christmas night that Uncle Mike appeared. And it changed the whole day!

The Christmas dinner was a delight with all of Abigail's favorite foods. And after dinner all the grownups sat in the big, easy chairs, or stretched out on the sofas before the warm fire in the fireplace and napped.

Morrison came over to see Caroline, and they sat in the sunroom. Even though it was a little chilly, they didn't seem to mind.

Robert, Abigail, and Gloria went down to the playroom in the basement. They played ping-pong for a while, and after a while Mary Margaret came over.

While Robert and Gloria were finishing a game, Abby and Mary Margaret went back into Father's workroom. Mary Margaret went over to a stack of calendars on Father's desk. She held up a big calendar with the picture of a beautiful Indian Maiden kneeling at a campfire, against the background of a beautiful forest. "What is this?"

"Oh, that is the calendar with Father's company name, the Empire Insurance Company, which they give to their customers," Abby replied.

"Oh, it is so beautiful…I can't understand their giving them away." Mary Margaret answered as she admired the calendar.

Abby held up another larger one, "See, here are bigger ones, too."

"I would think they could sell them…"

Abby hesitated a moment as she thought, and then she called to Robert. "Robert! I have a great idea!"

"Just a minute…until we finish this game… it's almost over." Robert answered.

Abby took one of the calendars and held it up for Robert to see as she asked, "Why don't we sell these calendars? I bet we could make some money."

"What do you mean?" Robert asked.

Abby explained her idea to Robert as Gloria and Mary Margaret listened, and they decided to do it!

They each took an armful of calendars and started out to sell them door to door. They decided to charge a nickel for the large calendar and three cents for the smaller. Robert and Gloria took the east side of the street, and Abby and Mary Margaret the west side of the street.

Their sales were marvelously successful. Almost everyone bought a calendar. The timing was right with 1933 just a week away, almost everyone had a need for a new calendar. The calendars were beautiful, and on Christmas afternoon their neighbors were feeling happy and open to buying from their young friends.

A couple of hours later, they met back home in the basement. Abby and Mary Margaret put their earnings on the ping-pong table, and when Robert and Gloria came in they added their money to the pile. Together they had a total of $1.84. Abby got a piece of paper and a pencil, and when she divided $1.84 by 4, they each got 46 cents!

With glee, they each pocketed their profits, and Mary Margaret went home.

All in all it was a happy day; that is, until Uncle Mike returned at about nine in the evening. All the food had been put away. Abby, Robert, Gram, and Father were playing Chinese checkers at the dining room table, and Caroline and Morrison were playing double solitaire at the other end of the table.

Mother and Uncle George were playing a game of chess at the chess table. Aunt Hester sat by the fireside knitting, and Gloria was sitting at her feet reading one of her new books.

Suddenly there was the noise of stomping feet at the back door. Robert joked, "Sounds like Santa Claus…he's just a little late!"

Father looked up sharply, glanced at Mother, who looked up and caught his eye. Quickly he pushed back from the table, almost knocking over the Chinese checkerboard, and strode to the back door. Mother also got up and followed Father.

All the games ceased, and everyone sat motionless as they listened. But there was nothing to hear, that is, except the slamming of the back door as Father walked out on the back stoop. The sounds of voices rose and fell, and then silence broken by the sound of footsteps on the back steps. Mother and Father walked back into the house.

Mother's face looked white and drained. She looked as if she would like to say something, but couldn't. Father stood in the middle of the hallway between the dining room and living room, and in a very flat voice, announced, "Mike will not be living here any longer, and none of us will be talking to him."

With that he walked back to the dining room table, straightened the Chinese checkerboard, and resumed the game.

Chapter Thirteen

Gloria always told her mother everything! So, of course, it wasn't a surprise that she told her mother about the sale of the calendars. With all the excitement of Christmas, Abigail had almost forgotten how angry she was with Gloria, but when Gloria tattled about the calendar sales, Abigail was really mad!

It was the next day after Christmas when Mother, in her no-nonsense voice, called, "Abigail and Robert, come here immediately!" From the tone of her voice, it was clear that they were in trouble. Gloria had not wasted any time in tattling!

Mother was sitting at the dining room table as she said, "Sit down. I need to talk with both of you."

Abby looked at Robert and Robert at Abby, as they stood uneasily in front of Mother. Mother was frowning and she looked squarely at Abby and then at Robert. "I would like you to tell me what you did with Father's calendars," Mother said sharply.

Abby took a deep breath and looked at Robert. It was such a terrible day. The house seemed filled with gloom. Not at all like a happy day after Christmas. Uncle Mike's gifts were still under the Christmas tree, but he was gone. The door to the stairway to the third floor was closed and locked!

Mother's eyes looked red as if she had been crying, and her voice sounded tired. "Gloria said you sold the calendars."

Abigail closed her eyes tightly as she thought... "Gloria! Gloria said!" She knew from the tone of her mother's voice that they shouldn't have sold the calendars, but she didn't understand why.

"We thought it was a good idea," Robert protested. "We made $1.84, and everyone was glad to get a new calendar." Abby nodded in agreement; she was so glad to have Robert speak up.

Mother explained slowly and patiently that the calendars were free to be given away to advertise Father's insurance company.

And so Robert and Abigail had to go to every house where they had sold a calendar to return the money, apologize, and tell them to keep the calendar. It was very embarrassing!

And Glor-i-a didn't have to go to return the money. She didn't even give her money back!

The days were short, and darkness came early. To Abigail it seemed that there was time only to go to school. And the evenings were not so much fun, as they had been when Uncle Mike was there. She wondered if he were cold wherever he was, and she knew Justin was cold every night when she let him out to go to sleep in the playhouse.

Gram usually played solitaire with Abby for a while in the evening, but Gloria did her homework each evening and never played games. Sometimes Robert and Gram and Abby played Chinese checkers, but everyone else was too busy to play with them.

Sometimes Mother asked, "Abigail, do you not have any homework?"

And she didn't really. She did all her work at school. But Mother glanced over at Gloria bent over her writing, working so industriously. It was downright sickening! Gloria was always doing extra credit work and copying her work over so it was just perfect!

Abigail and Mary Margaret became more and more disgusted with Gloria. She sat in the front row and always raised her hand every time Mrs. Lingle asked a question. Worse yet she always knew the answer to everything! And after a while, it was Gloria that the teacher asked to take notes to the principal, and to pass out the books, and to do anything special!

When report cards came at the end of the semester, of course, Gloria had all A+'s. Mary Margaret and Abby both looked at their own grades, and then they walked slowly home and let Gloria get far ahead of them. Of course, Gloria was in a hurry to get home to tell her mother.

"Let's go to the vacant lot," said Abigail.

Mary Margaret hesitated, "It's pretty cold."

"I know, but I just can't stand to go home with Gloria now."

"You don't mean to stay in the woods?" Mary Margaret asked quickly.

"No, of course not," Abby answered impatiently. "It's only so we can give Gloria a little time, maybe she'll go up to her parents' room with her mother, and then I can go home with my report card."

The two girls turned the corner and ran down to the woods in the vacant lot. They climbed up on the big rock and sat down, pulling their coats around them to keep warm. Abby took out her report card and studied the grades. It really wasn't that her grades were that bad, it was just that Gloria's were that good!

"Mary Margaret, what did you get in Language Arts?"

"I got a B. That's pretty good. I came up from a C+ last time. What did you get in math?"

Abby looked at her grade card. "I got a B in everything except Science, and I got an A in Science."

Mary Margaret shook her head as she said, "Abby, I think that's pretty good. You shouldn't worry about going home."

"You just don't know how it is to live with Gloria. She studies every night, and she got all A+'s!" Abigail took a deep breath.

"Yeah, I know she is a pain," Mary Margaret agreed and then she changed the subject. "Why don't we play pretend...pretend that we are lost in a forest and no one knows where we are and we have to find a way home."

"But how did we get lost?" Abigail asked.

Mary Margaret frowned a little as she thought, "Maybe we live a long way from town out on a ranch in the country and we had to go to get some supplies from town...and it started to snow, and we lost our way."

They left their books and report cards on the big rock and started walking along the snowy paths and under low hanging tree branches as they pretended they were trying to find their way home. As they played, it got darker and darker, and they sat down in a little clearing and pretended they had a campfire to keep warm.

The game went on, as each girl kept making up more parts to the story until finally they came to the edge of the woods on the street on the back side of the vacant lot. When they came out, it was so dark that Mary Margaret said, "We had better hurry home! It's so dark and late; we are going to be in trouble." And they both started running.

Mary Margaret was so right! They were in trouble!

When Abby came running up the steps of the front porch, her mother was standing in the doorway and demanded, "Where have you been?"

"Mary Margaret and I stopped to play on the way home from school…"

Mother didn't give her a chance to finish, "You know you are to come straight home from school! Your father is going to be very upset about this!"

Abby got a cold chill right straight through her chest and her stomach. She hadn't thought about this much trouble! "Oh, don't tell Father!"

"Of course, your father has to know. Where have you been?"

Abigail had a terrible time answering. She knew she shouldn't lie, but she also knew that she was going to be in big trouble if her parents knew she had been in the woods. She gulped. Then she said almost under her breath, "Mary

Margaret and I just stopped…on the way and played a little."

"Played what and where and with whom?" demanded Mother.

"No one else…just us…"

Mother persisted, "And where?"

Abigail took a another deep breath, "In the woods…"

"In the woods at the vacant lot?" Mother asked.

"You know that you are not to go there to play! Now go up to your room!"

Abby was glad to run up to her room away from Mother's questions, but as she reached the door she suddenly hoped that Gloria wouldn't be there.

No such luck! Gloria was stretched out on her bed reading. Abigail flounced down on her bed and thew her coat on the floor. She didn't cry, but she sure felt like it.

Gloria didn't say anything for a little while and then she said, "Did you show your mother your report card?"

Abigail sat straight up in bed…and then she remembered that she had left her books and the report card in the woods!

Chapter Fourteen

Abby leaped to her feet and threw her coat on.

"What are you doing?" asked Gloria.

"Never mind," Abby replied, "and don't you tell on me!"

"Tell on you! I don't know what you are doing, so how could I tell?" Gloria answered haughtily.

Abby ran down the back stairs, looked carefully into the kitchen where her mother and Gram were fixing dinner, and then tiptoed out the side entrance. She ran down to the playhouse and let Justin out.

As he came bounding out, she had a strange feeling that someone was in the playhouse. She was in such a hurry to get back to the woods to get her report card and books that she didn't even stop to think about whether there really was someone there. But she thought about it later, when she discovered who it was.

Although it was only five thirty, it was quite dark. The sky was cloudy and as gray as if it were full of snow just ready for a blizzard. Abby and Justin ran down the back walk to the alley. She had to hurry! It was only a half-hour or so until dinner time, and she really would be in deep trouble if she weren't back for dinner.

As she ran down the alley, she shivered not only from the cold wind, but also the scary feeling in the pit of her stomach. It seemed so dark, and she felt so alone as she ran along. And then when she got to the corner she ran squarely into a big, dark figure who put his arms out as he caught her!

Her heart pounded, and her throat tightened, and she couldn't even scream! She was so relieved when she looked up and it was Robert.

"Abby, what are you doing?" asked Robert.

"Oh, Rob, I am in such trouble…Mother's mad at me…and I lost my report card…and she sent me to my room…and I…"

Robert couldn't help laughing at Abby, "Wait a minute! Mother is mad at you because you lost your report card?"

"Not exactly…she doesn't know I lost my report card…and I have to find it before she finds out! She's mad because I didn't come straight home from school…and went to the woods to play…and she sent me up to my room…which is where I am supposed to be…but I left my books and report card in the woods at the vacant lot." Abby explained breathlessly.

"O.K., now I see." Robert was serious as he went on. "So you have to go to the vacant lot to find it. Well, it's too dark for you to go alone. That was pretty dumb. I'll go with you and we'll hurry back."

Abby drew a deep breath. It was so good to have Robert go with her. They ran along together with Justin at their heels. They ran through the back of the woods to the big boulder where Abby had put her books. And there they were! She grabbed her books with the report card, and they started to leave, when Robert stumbled and almost fell.

"Come on, Rob," Abby cried. "We have to hurry."

The tall dark branches overhead swayed and creaked in the wind. The dark shadows in the woods looked ominous as if there was someone hiding behind each tree. The woods were frightening and spooky in the dark.

"Wait a minute, Abby. Come here!" Rob called as he pulled back a small tree trunk and brushed away leaves covering a piece of furniture. It was a cabinet.

Robert's face was serious as he pushed back a little farther and felt around. Then he uncovered a sink. "A kitchen sink!"

"Oh, Rob, let's get out of here! Maybe these are from the Allen's house. Maybe the robbers who broke into their house stole these…. They must hide things here! Maybe they are here now!"

Abby's heart started to pound. She grabbed Robert's hand, "Come on! Let's go!"

"You're right! Let's get out of here! Do you have your books?"

Abby nodded and showed him her armful of books. "Come on!" And together they ran out onto the street, and Abby didn't take a deep breath until they had run clear down to the corner from the lot.

Abby ran on, but Robert started to walk. "It's all right now, Abby."

They walked along together silently. Abby's thoughts were racing. "I don't understand. Why would robbers take those things out of the Allen's house, and then just leave them in the vacant lot?"

Robert's thoughts were racing also, but he answered slowly, "I think the thieves must hide these things when they steal them, and then come back later and get them."

"But why would anyone take a kitchen sink?" asked Abby.

"I guess they would sell it for money," Robert frowned as he was thinking. But by this time they were almost home, and he told Abby, "If you don't want to get caught, you run through the yard and in the side door. I'll go in the kitchen. When I come in they'll see me and not notice you going up the backstairs."

Abby opened the side door quietly, and when she heard Robert stamping his feet as he went in the back door, she darted up the backstairs.

She ran into her room, flung off her coat and just dropped it on the floor as she put her books on the bed. Then she flipped on the light. Gloria wasn't there. That was a relief! At least she didn't have to come up with any explanations.

She had just stretched out on her bed when she heard footsteps coming up the stairs and within moments Mother opened the door. "Abigail, you may come down to dinner now." Then Mother looked at her rumpled coat on the floor and the stack of books on the bed. She sighed and said, "Abigail, I do not understand why it is so difficult for you to just hang up your coat and put your books on the desk."

Abby took a deep breath. Her cheeks were still cold from the outside air. She was glad her mother was just noticing the mess.

Although Mother looked at her sharply, her voice was quiet as she said, "I understand you got your report card today. Did that have anything to do with your not coming straight home after school?"

Abigail sat straight up. "I am sorry, Mother," and she truly was. "It wasn't the report card exactly, but kind of. Do you want to see it?"

Mother watched as Abby pulled her report card from her literature book. Together they looked at the card.

"Abigail, this is not a bad report. Some of your grades have even improved. With a little more study, you could improve even more."

Abby blurted, "But Gloria got all A+'s!

Mother said, "I know…. Aunt Hester told me."

Abby felt sad, as if she had let her mother down.

Then Mother put her arm around Abby and squeezed hard. "Abby, I would like you to study more so that you could learn more for you, not for grades to make me happy, or to have to make better grades than Gloria. But you are just fine, and I love you very much." Mother got up and put her hand out to Abby. "Now let's go down for dinner. Then after dinner you can show your report to your father, and I am sure he will be pleased."

Chapter Fifteen

And then everything started happening so
fast that Abigail had trouble remembering it
all. It was the next night when she let Justin out
for the night and she had gone out to put him
in the playhouse. She was putting him in his
blanket, and as she was wrapping it around him,
she thought she heard a noise from the upstairs.
She gasped because she immediately thought
of the thieves. A chill came over her, and she
was covered with goosebumps. Then she heard,
"Abby, don't be afraid," and Uncle Mike climbed
down the ladder from the second floor.

Abby felt a wave of relief, but she didn't know
what to say! She felt a little strange, almost afraid,
but as she looked at Uncle Mike with his warm
smile, she knew she did not need to be afraid.

"What?…Why?" She stammered. She had
trouble getting the words out to ask, "What are

you doing here?" And then she was embarrassed because she sounded so rude.

"Sit down, Abby." Uncle Mike motioned for her to sit on the blanket on the floor by Justin, and he also sat down on the floor. Slowly and quietly he started to talk. "I started sleeping here sometimes because I didn't have any money, and I had nowhere to go."

"I am sorry, Uncle Mike!" Abby said quickly. She felt so bad. "Mother and Father were mean."

"No! No!" Uncle Mike said, shaking his head. "Your mother and father were very good to me. It was my fault that I had to leave, but I will talk more about that later. Your mother and father are very good to everybody."

Uncle Mike patted Justin who lay down beside him, and then he continued to explain slowly as if he were choosing his words very carefully. "I have a little job now. I am trying to save my wages to buy some decent clothes so that I can get a better paying job. I have an offer to work as a shoe salesman, just as soon as I can buy a suit. So I started staying here instead of spending the money for a room."

"But where do you eat?" Abby asked.

"There are soup kitchens where food is served to people who have only a little or no money."

Abigail scrambled to her feet. She didn't know how she felt about Uncle Mike. He seemed just like he always did. "I've got to go. Mother will wonder why I haven't come back into the house."

"Abigail, you must do what you think is right. If you feel you need to tell your folks I am here, that's all right." Uncle Mike said seriously as she turned to go out the door.

Abigail knew it wouldn't be all right and that her folks would make him leave. As she walked slowly up the back path, she decided it really wouldn't hurt anything if he stayed in the playhouse a little while longer, and then he could get a good job and leave. And so she didn't tell!

Abigail felt like she was getting in deeper and deeper with so many things she couldn't tell. She tried to make herself feel better that she wasn't lying. She just wasn't telling! And she felt like Gloria was looking at her all the time trying to find out all the things Abigail knew and wasn't telling.

Gloria watched when she and Robert were talking. They had to whisper, and Gloria knew there was something up. Robert and Abigail knew they couldn't tell about what they had found in the woods, because Abigail wasn't supposed to be there. So they decided that Rob would go down the next day, and then he could tell what he had seen. But when he went through the woods the next afternoon, the sink and the cabinet were gone! There were scraped places through the snow where several things had been drug out of the woods. So now there was nothing to tell!

Robert continued to look in the woods almost every day. Oftentimes after he had delivered his papers he would cut back through the vacant lot. One day after a week or two, he saw something. Again, it was carefully covered over with branches and snow piled over it, but it was a little difficult to disguise a bathtub!

"A bathtub!" Robert exclaimed to himself as he saw it. "Who would want a bathtub?" He pulled back the branches, which were lying across the bathtub, and saw two stained glass windows in the tub…and also several planks of oak paneling. Quickly he ran out of the woods and down the street.

Caroline was standing in the kitchen drinking a cup of hot chocolate, and their father and mother were at breakfast when he came running in the back door. "Dad!" Robert shouted, "There are some stolen things in the vacant lot!"

"Wait a minute, Rob. What do you mean? What things?"

"A bathtub…some windows, and paneling," Robert answered breathlessly.

"A bathtub!" Caroline exclaimed sarcastically. "Who steals a bathtub?"

Father frowned as he asked, "What do you mean? What were you doing in the vacant lot?"

"Just taking a short cut, and I have seen other strange things before…"

Abigail heard the commotion and ran down the stairs and into the kitchen, just in time to hear her father say, "We'll go down and check and call the police."

Mother shook her head. "What a terrible thing. I wonder where these things came from?"

Father took a last sip of coffee, wiped his mouth on his napkin, and started to get up. "These are bad times. Thieves are ripping houses apart to sell anything they can find to sell."

The police came after Abigail had gone to school. Father said that Robert could stay and talk to the police, but everyone else should go on to school. Abigail wanted to say she knew something about this, too, but she knew she dare not.

Chapter Sixteen

The police checked the Allen's house, and sure enough, the bathtub and the sink had been ripped out of the house! Mr. Allen came to see the amount of the damage, and he was sickened by what he saw.

"We thought we were doing the best thing to move in with SaraLou," but he shook his head as he said sadly. "It looks like it is going to cost us more. Who would have thought thieves would tear a house apart!"

Father and Uncle George were also shocked. "We thought we could see anything going on at your house, but obviously the thief is very clever." They assured Mr. Allen that they would watch very carefully so that nothing else would be stolen…or to try to catch the thief.

Uncle George offered to repair and reinstall the plumbing that had been removed. "We would like to rent your house, just as soon as I can get established in a job again."

Abby didn't spend much time in the playhouse, but she did take Justin out every night. Sometimes she took some of the leftovers from dinner. Uncle Mike usually wasn't there. When he wasn't, she left the food at the top of the ladder where Justin couldn't get it. When Uncle Mike was there, they talked some…but not a lot.

One time Uncle Mike looked very serious and said slowly as if it were difficult to get the words out. "Abby, I want to tell you something." He paused and then went on, "I am sure you know that I was drunk and that was the reason your parents asked me to leave."

Abigail didn't know what to say. She was standing by the door, and she started to leave.

"Wait a minute, Abby. I want to say…they were right. I am not a bad person, but I have made many mistakes. And drinking was the worst. I know now, and I am trying…really trying not to ever drink again."

Abby felt uncomfortable, and she didn't know what to say so she didn't say anything. She didn't know exactly what Uncle Mike was trying to say.

Uncle Mike could see how uncomfortable Abby was, and he said, "That's enough of that."

Abby ran on back into the house. Gloria was standing at the back door watching her as she came in.

"What's going on?" Abby asked Gloria.

"All the grownups are listening to President Roosevelt's speech on the radio," Gloria said and then asked, "What were you doing?"

"Oh, I just took Justin out to the playhouse," and then Abby added in a mean tone of voice, "since he can't sleep inside anymore!"

After the President's speech was over, all the family sat around the radio, which was now turned off. They talked about what the new President had said. Father said, "I think we are on the right track."

Uncle George nodded his head as he agreed, "I do believe we are going to start going forward."

Mother added, "I so firmly agree that the only thing we have to be afraid of is fear itself! With confidence and working together, I am sure everything is going to be all right again."

"I certainly hope so," Aunt Hester said. "I am looking toward the day when we can rent the Allen's house. It will be good for all of us when we can have our own home again, but still be close enough that Gloria and Abby can be together."

Abby thought to herself, "Thanks a lot!" It would be fine with her if Gloria moved clear across town!

"It would be such a help to the Allens to be able to have the income from renting their house," Father added. "Not to mention the relief from the worry of the thievery of anything or everything in the house!"

But in only days everything changed. The new President closed all the banks! To begin with, Father and Uncle George were puzzled by the move, but they thought perhaps this action by the President was necessary. But then it became very clear that no one had any money and no way to get any money! And perhaps the banks might not open again.

The supper table was quiet as everyone ate in silence. The bean soup was delicious and hearty with onions and carrots and chile sauce, just the way Abby loved it. And the cornbread tasted so good with hot, melted butter. Robert was out doing his evening collections on his newspaper route. He had eaten his soup and cornbread early so that he could make his collections in the early evening.

"I'll be glad when Rob gets back. It is so cold outside," Mother said.

The wind, whipping around the outside of the house, howled and whistled weirdly. The white, heavy snow whirled and hit against the dining room window with a dull, thudding sound. Abby wondered if Uncle Mike were in the playhouse, and she hoped he was warm enough.

As soon as Father finished his soup, he pushed his chair back from the table and announced,

"As soon as everyone has finished and the table is cleared, I would like the family to gather in the living room. We have some things we need to discuss."

Abby looked at Father's serious face, and it made her feel a little uneasy. She wondered what he wanted to talk about. She hoped he didn't know about Uncle Mike.

When everyone was finished, Mother, Gram, and Aunt Hester started to clear the dishes to the kitchen. Mother turned around to say, "Come on, girls, each of you bring out the dishes."

Abby turned to her sister, who was doing nothing and said, "You, too, Caroline!"

"You too, Abby," Caroline retorted, but they both noticed Gloria walking the other way. When Gloria saw Abby and Caroline watching her, she picked up her own dishes and followed them into the kitchen.

The grandfather clock chimed eight times, and the entire family gathered in the living room. The orange flames in the fireplace danced, but the shadows darted about eerily on the ceiling. "Can't we turn on a light?" asked Caroline almost peevishly.

"Turn on the light beside you," Father answered, "but it is important that we conserve electricity…and now more than ever."

He stood by the fireplace and looked about the family circle. "I don't want to sound glum, but we do have a serious matter we need to talk about."

Uncle George nodded his head, as he seemed to know what Father was about to say. Abby felt anxious. She had never seen her father look so serious…and never with the whole family together like this. She felt worried. She hoped this wasn't about Uncle Mike.

"We all know that President Roosevelt has closed the banks, and we really didn't know what that would mean to us. But now it is all too clear. We have only a very little money in the house and no way to get any more. What little money we do have is in the bank, and the bank is closed. We cannot get our money out to pay our mortgage on the house or the electric bill…thankfully we don't have a telephone bill…not even any money to buy food."

Abby didn't understand why the banks were closed, or why they didn't have any money at all, but she did know it was no time for kids to ask questions.

Gram shook her head, as she said vehemently, "I knew I made a mistake when I voted for that man!"

Father frowned, "I don't know…I just don't know!" In the shadows, the lines on his forehead looked deep, and his mouth was firm and tightly drawn.

Mother's cheeks looked pink. She pursed her lips a little and then said in a very flat tone of voice, "I am sure we will find the money we need some way."

"Martha, I wish I were as sure." Father answered.

Just then Robert burst in the front door, bringing a blast of winter snow in the door with him. He stamped his feet loudly as he came into the living room. He looked around with some surprise at the somber family group. Then he blurted, "I collected the newspaper money from only two people...old Mrs. Trimpe and the Johnsons. No one else had any money! All those rich people on Washington Boulevard, and no one had 25 cents to pay for their weekly newspaper!"

Caroline looked at Rob in disbelief. "That can't be! The people who live on Washington Boulevard and Meridian Street are the richest people in town!"

Uncle George shook his head as he said sadly, "It is unbelievable! The whole country is at a standstill."

Robert interrupted, which wasn't like him, "Wouldn't you think those people would have enough money in the house to pay the newsboy?" And then he said, "What am I going to do? I have to pay the News Company for the papers."

Father repeated, "This then is what we are facing. We have bills we have to pay...and no money!"

Chapter Seventeen

Father seemed to dismiss the family group as he said, "We will talk more about this tomorrow… and maybe for several tomorrows."

"All right, girls, it's time for bed," Mother said to Abby and Gloria.

Gloria went on upstairs, but Abby ran to the kitchen. She quickly took two big pieces of cornbread, wrapped them in a napkin, and ran out the back door. She grabbed her old play coat from the hook on the back porch and ran to the playhouse. She lowered her head as she plowed through the heavy snow, and the wind whipped the wet snowflakes into her face.

As she pushed open the crude door, she saw Uncle Mike wrapped in blankets sitting on the floor with Justin snuggled up to him.

"Abby, what is this? You shouldn't be out on a night like this!"

"I brought you some cornbread," she said as she handed him the wrapped cornbread, which was still a little warm.

As he took it, Mike shook his head, "The folks will wonder where you are."

Abby sat down on the cold floor and shivered as she wrapped her coat tightly around her. "I don't think they will even know."

"What do you mean…they won't know?"

"We don't have any money," Abby blurted out. "I don't understand. Robert says even the very rich people over on Meridian Street don't have enough money to pay their newspaper boy."

Uncle Mike was quiet, and then he answered slowly and thoughtfully. "Oh…because the banks are closed down…so you mean any money your folks have is in the bank…and now..."

"Father says we don't have any money to pay our bills…or to buy groceries…or anything!"

"Abby, it will only be for a short time. Go on back into the house." Uncle Mike's voice was reassuring.

"All right," Abby replied. She knew she had to get back into the house before she was missed. She clutched her coat around her as she stepped out into the swirling snow. As she came out of the door she saw Gloria looking out of their bedroom window, and she knew that Gloria had seen her. What she didn't know was that Uncle Mike had come to the door to close it after Abby, and Gloria saw him, too!

Abby was right that none of the grownups knew she had been out of the house. They were all still talking in the living room. As she ducked through the back hallway, Abby could hear their voices. She heard Robert saying that many people wouldn't even answer the door…and those who did told him to come back next week. Caroline said firmly, "I am sure that Morrison's family has money. They are very rich!"

"They didn't even answer the door," Robert replied.

Abby had such a hollow feeling. She didn't understand how it was that nobody had any money. Maybe they had some money, but they didn't want to spend it. She walked up the stairs slowly as she thought how strange everything was. She didn't say anything as she walked into her bedroom, and Gloria didn't say anything to her either. It wasn't that they were mad at each other. They just didn't have anything to say. After Abby got into her pajamas, she peeked into Gram's room, but it was dark. Gram was still downstairs with the others.

The next morning the house was very chilly, but the kitchen was warm with the breakfast cooking. When Abby came in, Caroline was standing drinking her hot chocolate and saying, "I don't understand why the house has to be so cold! We didn't suddenly run out of coal for the furnace."

"That's right," Father answered, "but we need to use it carefully so that we don't run out of coal before the winter is over…since we don't know when we can buy more."

Mary Margaret, Gloria, and Abby ran and skipped through the snow on the way to school. The sun was shining, the sky was blue, and the snow underfoot creaked and squeaked in the deep cold. Everything in the day seemed just the same. School was like every other school day, and the cold winter day was just like any other cold day in March, but Abby felt as if there were a cloud over her. She felt a strange feeling of anxiety, but she didn't quite know what she was anxious about. And then she would think, and she knew.

At dinner there were candles on the table. That wasn't so unusual because oftentimes they had candles at dinner, but this night was unusual because they didn't have the electric lights on.

Caroline interrupted the silence, "I don't understand. What are we gaining by not using electricity?"

Abby felt Caroline was being a pain complaining about everything…the phone… the heat…the electricity, but Abby didn't really understand either.

Father answered patiently but firmly. "We have to pay for all the electricity we use. If we can't pay, the company turns off the electricity. It is better that we save now than to be cut off later."

"They wouldn't do that! " Caroline exclaimed, "They can't turn off everyone's electricity!"

Father's mouth turned down at the corners as he said, "Believe me, they can…and they will!"

Robert said under his breath to Abby, "Just like the old days before Tom Edison!"

The doorbell rang just as the family was finishing dinner. It was Morrison at the front door, and Caroline, as usual, got out of doing the dishes.

"Come, let's play some rummy," said Gram as the table was cleared. And so Gram, Caroline, Morrison, and Uncle George sat down to play cards. Gram placed the candle to the side as she dealt the cards.

Caroline said, "We're playing by candlelight to save electricity."

Morrison laughed, "And isn't it romantic!"

Gram smiled and turned her head just so, "I've never looked better," she joked, and her dark eyes shone in the flickering light.

They played a hand of cards and Morrison said, "This is so good to be able to have a good time playing cards, even if everyone is hurting for money. This is much better than my house. Dad has closed the entire house except for the kitchen and his study. Mother is sitting in the kitchen, and that's different because when we had maids, she never went into the kitchen. Dad sits at his desk in the study shuffling papers. I go up to my room, but it's freezing!"

Caroline was shocked but, in a teasing voice, she said, "What's new? Our upstairs is freezing, too!"

Abby looked about. The fire in the fireplace was warm and inviting. Mother was working her crossword puzzle. Gloria was studying as always. Aunt Hester and Uncle George were playing double solitaire, and Robert and Father were sitting at the little living room desk going over Robert's newspaper accounts.

Abby got up quietly, went through the kitchen, picked up a piece of peach cobbler, put it on a plate, and ran out the back door with her playcoat half on. Justin danced along beside her, teasing for the food she had in her hand. "Oh Justin, this isn't for you!" The moon was high in the sky and laid a silver stream of light across the snow.

Uncle Mike opened the door and Justin ran in barking happily and wagging his tail merrily.

"Shh...quiet, Justin...don't make so much noise," Abby scolded.

"How are things in the house?" Uncle Mike asked.

"I guess, just the same. We had to turn the electricity off and the heat down."

Uncle Mike looked quickly out the door at the house and asked with alarm, "You mean you have no electricity?"

"No, we just don't have any money to pay the bill. So Father thinks we should not use very much, and he's saving the coal so that what we have in the coal bin will last through the winter."

Abby started to leave.

"Wait a minute, Abby." Uncle Mike went back to his blanket folded neatly in the corner and pulled out a small packet tied with a string. "Here, you take this to your parents. But you must promise you will not tell where you got it."

Abby automatically took the packet, but she didn't understand, "What do you mean?"

Uncle Mike said quietly, "Your folks helped me when I needed it. They need money now… so please give this to them."

Abby looked down at the neat package.

"There's a little money in the package. I have been working, and I have saved all that I made to buy that suit for a better job. But I can wait a little longer…." Then Uncle Mike repeated sternly, "But you must promise!"

Abby looked at the package and then at Uncle Mike. She didn't know what to say. "I don't think I should take this…"

Uncle Mike pushed her out the door. "Just give it to your father."

Abby ran back to the house and up to her room. She put the package under her pillow. And then she thought her mother might come into the room to make the bed, and she looked for a safer place. Then she heard Gloria on the stairs, and she quickly put it in her bottom drawer.

Chapter Eighteen

And, so, that is how Abby had the money to give to the family. She thought a great deal about how she should give it to Father. She could have just placed it on his desk…and maybe that is what she should have done. She had left it in the bottom drawer when she went to school, and after school she ran up to make sure it was still there. She carefully placed it in her pocket just before dinner. She felt the weight of it in her sweater pocket as she was setting the table. She looked at Father sitting in his chair by the fire and started to give it to him then, but she didn't quite know what to say.

So after dinner, when Gram gave the money to Father, it seemed like the right time. And she had felt so good that she could help out, too.

But it hadn't turned out right! And now she was in trouble, and if she told, Uncle Mike would be, too. And that wasn't right after he had tried to help.

For a very long time Abby lay on her bed sometimes crying and sometimes just thinking about all the things that had happened this winter. Abby heard footsteps on the stairs. She hoped it wasn't Gloria. She didn't want to have to talk to her!

And it wasn't. The door opened slowly, and her father came in. Darkness filled the room, and the dim light from the hall around him made him look like a shadow.

Father came into the room quietly and turned on the lamp by Abby's bed. He looked at Abby's rumpled hair and her eyes wet with tears. He put his arms around her and smoothed back her hair. "Abby, I know you think you were doing the right thing, and we do appreciate your desire to help the family, but it is important that we know where the money came from."

Abby felt so awful. "I can't tell, Father. I promised that I wouldn't tell!"

Father helped Abby sit up against the head of her bed, and he moved back so that he could see her better. Very seriously he said, "I know it is important to keep your word. Promises are important, and in most cases, I would not ask you to break your promise. I hope you understand that…" he hesitated, took a deep breath, and went on. "But in this case, it is even more important. There has been thievery in the neighborhood. If you found the money, it just could have been stolen money, and I know you wouldn't want us to use money that had been gotten dishonestly."

"Oh, Father, it has nothing to do with the robbery. I didn't find it. Uncle Mike gave it to me to give to you," Abby blurted out. And then she had done it! She had broken her promise to Uncle Mike, and she felt so terrible!

Father's dark brown eyes looked even darker as he looked straight at Abby as he asked, "Where did you see your Uncle Mike?"

Abby gulped and knew she had to tell the truth. "Uncle Mike was sleeping in the playhouse."

"How did you know this?" Father's question was sharp.

"I saw him when I took Justin out for the night."

"Which night was this?"

Abby felt a little warm despite the chilly room. She felt that everything she said was just getting her into more trouble. "He's been sleeping there for a while."

Father's eyebrows lifted in surprise. "In the cold?"

Abby went on quickly to explain that Uncle Mike was working, and he was sleeping in the playhouse to try to save his money to buy a suit so he could get a better job.

Father's expression didn't change. "Why did he give you this money?"

"He knew we needed money to pay our bills."

"You told him this?"

"Well, not exactly. He kind of guessed. Father, he really wanted to help. He said you had been good to him."

Father was quiet for a moment, and then he said, "Abby, you really aren't at fault. I know you thought you were helping," he paused and said slowly almost as if he were thinking aloud. "But I wonder how Mike got that money."

The next morning when Abby went down for breakfast, Mother was standing at the stove stirring scrambled eggs in the hot skillet. She turned and put her arm around Abby and hugged her. Abby was surprised, but it felt good.

It was a long day. Abby took Justin out. He had slept in her room all night, and surprisingly Gloria hadn't said a thing about it. When she got to the playhouse, it seemed bare. Uncle Mike's blanket was folded up neatly at the top of the stairs, and there were two bowls on top of the blanket.

Abby took the bowls and ran back to the house to put them in the kitchen. As she went on to the back porch she could hear her mother and father talking in rather loud tones. "I have to know that it was not Mike who took the things from Allen's house and sold them to get that money," Father said.

And Mother answered in an equally determined tone, "Mike has made mistakes, but I know he would not steal…and definitely not from our neighbors!"

"The fact remains the source of the money is unknown, and someone has been stealing, ripping sinks and bathtubs from the house to be sold for money."

Mother's voice was sharp as she said, "Can you imagine one man carrying a bathtub out of a house…and a block down to a vacant lot…really!"

Abby left the bowls on the porch and ran down to Mary Margaret's house. Her eyes were hot with tears. How could they think Uncle Mike would do such an awful thing!

She ran to the door and asked Cecilia, Mary Margaret's sister, if Mary Margaret could come out to play, and soon Mary Margaret ran down the steps to where Abby and Justin were waiting.

Mary Margaret looked at Abby's red eyes. "Have you been crying?"

Abby shook her head. "Come on, let's go to the vacant lot."

"I thought you weren't supposed to," answered Mary Margaret.

"Well," Abby sighed. "I think it's all right in the daytime, besides we have to go someplace where we can talk."

They walked deep into the woods and sat down on a log. The winter sunlight fell through the branches in pale patches of dim light. And Abby told Mary Margaret the story.

"Gosh, I would think they would be so glad to have the money," Mary Margaret said.

"I thought so, too, but now I'm in deep trouble, and they think Uncle Mike stole the money," Abby replied woefully.

Very softly Mary Margaret asked, "You don't think he did, do you?"

"Mary Margaret!" Abby exclaimed. "Of course he didn't!" But inwardly she wished she knew for sure.

"Sh...sh," Mary Margaret said quickly, and then she whispered, "I think I hear someone."

Quickly the two girls dived behind the log, and Abby held Justin down beside her. Justin's fur stood up on the back of his neck, and a low rumble of a growl rolled up in his throat. Abby put her head down on his and said into his ear, "Be quiet."

They could hear twigs crackling as if someone were walking into the front of the woods. And then they heard men's low voices. Mary Margaret peeked and whispered, "It's two men pulling off some branches back in the bushes."

It seemed forever. Abby was so cramped, but she knew she dared not move. Then she heard a gruff voice. "We need to make one more haul, and then we'll sell it all. We'll meet tonight at the vacant house up the street and clear it out once and for all."

Abby gasped...that would be the Allen's house. She had to see and so she peeked over the log carefully. She saw the backs of two men going out the front of the lot toward the street. One of the men was very tall with a scruffy cap and stringy brown hair, and the other, a short man in a grey jacket, walked with a limp.

Chapter Nineteen

"Oh, Mary Margaret, we have to catch those men tonight! Then everyone will know that Uncle Mike was telling the truth," Abby cried, as soon as she could breathe again.

Mary Margaret sat up straight. She frowned as she asked, "But how can you catch them? What are you going to do?"

Abby shook her head and bit her lip a little as she thought. Then she said slowly, "You and I could hide tonight and watch."

Mary Margaret took a deep breath. She did want to help, but that was scary. "Abby, we can't go out late at night." And then she added, "What if those men saw us?"

"All right! If you don't want to help!" Abby said in a cross tone as she scrambled to get to her feet.

"Oh, it isn't that I don't want to help…it's just…" Mary Margaret trailed off. She knew she didn't want to go spying at night.

"I know," Abby said. She did know that Mary Margaret was right. She knew that they couldn't go out late at night. And she couldn't think how they could catch two men. Her heart was racing. But she knew that catching those men was the answer, but she had to think how. "Come on, let's go home."

The day went by so slowly, even though Abby knew that she had a lot to do. First, she and Justin went to the playhouse to see whether Uncle Mike was there. But as soon as she walked in she knew he hadn't been there. The blanket was folded neatly just as it had been. Abby looked around the playhouse, and the only thing she saw was a scrap of paper on the floor, which she picked up. At the top it said "The Globe Cartage Company" and then "wages…$3.00."

Her spirits lifted, and she ran into the house. Mother was sitting in a rocking chair by the sunny dining room window with her mending in her hands.

"Mother, look what I found! This proves that Uncle Mike was working."

"What do you mean?" Mother asked.

And then she looked at the little slip of paper and her face seemed to relax some. She didn't smile, but neither did she frown when she demanded, "Where did you get this?"

And Abby told her about finding it in the playhouse, where Uncle Mike had been.

Afterward Abigail heard Mother telling Father about this clue that Mike was working. And she heard Father's reply, "Why didn't Mike tell us where the money came from?"

Mother's voice was sounded a little sharp, as she answered, "If you remember, he gave the money to Abby to bring to us with the promise that she wouldn't tell that he had given it. He didn't have to justify where he got the money!"

Then Father said so softly that Abby could hardly hear, "I know, Martha, but we have to be sure."

She thought and thought and then it came to her. Abby knew what she had to do! She had to find Robert, but she didn't know where he was. The day grew later and later, and Abby worried that she wasn't going to be able to do what she knew she had to do!

"Abby, set the table." Mother said.

Abby didn't even hear her she was so absorbed in her thoughts.

Mother repeated, "Abby…please set the table."

This time Abby heard and looked at Gloria who was just sitting reading her book. She started to complain that it was Gloria's turn to set the table, but decided it didn't matter. She just was anxious for Robert to come home. At last, Robert came in just before dinnertime. She ran to him and said, "Rob, I've got to talk to you."

Robert sighed and took off his coat and threw it on the floor with his newspaper collection book.

"Pick up your coat and hang it on the rack, Robert," Mother said.

"O.K....it's just that I can't collect enough money to pay my newspaper bill." He looked troubled as he ran his hands through his hair.

"Rob," Abby tried to get his attention.

"Oh, Abby, lay off. What do you want?" Robert said crossly.

Abigail saw Gloria look up from her book. She was waiting to hear what Abby was going to say.

Abby realized that she would just have to wait until later, but she felt so uneasy. She knew what they had to do, but she just could not do anything yet.

After dinner, which lasted forever, dishes were done, and Robert had disappeared. Abby looked all over for him and then she ran out to the playhouse again to see if Uncle Mike was there. And it was just as empty now as it had been in the morning.

Finally, she found Robert in the basement in Father's workroom, pouring over his newspaper collection records. "Rob, I have to talk to you! It is very important!" Then she told him about what she and Mary Margaret had seen and heard, and she asked him to help in what they had to do.

And so it was decided. Rob's bedroom was in the front of the house where he could see the Allen's house across the street, and he agreed that he would keep watch out of his window.

When Abigail and Gloria went up to bed they stopped in Gram's room as they usually did. Abby was so anxious that she could hardly sit still. Gram noticed and asked, "Abby, what on earth is the matter with you? You are like a spider on a hot griddle. Can't you sit still? I know it is chilly in here, but it isn't cold enough to make you shiver!"

"Gram, I'm tired. I think I'll go on to bed," Abby replied.

Gram looked a little suspicious. It wasn't often that Abby went to bed without being told to go and most particularly on a Saturday night.

Abby didn't undress. She just crawled under the covers and waited for Gloria to go to bed. And it seemed forever before Gloria did go to bed, and then Abby listened for Gloria's even breathing indicating that she had gone to sleep at last.

Shortly she heard a soft tapping at the door. Silently she crawled out of bed, and Robert was in the hall. Excitedly he whispered, "They're there! I know they are! I saw a light!"

Abby followed Robert into his room, and they both knelt by the window and watched. Abby's throat tightened, and she felt like her heart was pounding in her chest. At first she couldn't see anything, and then a shadowy light went past the front window like the beam of a flashlight.

"Come on, we've got to go…before they get away," Abigail said urgently as she pulled at Rob's sleeve. Stealthily they slipped into the hall. The light was out in Gram's room so they knew she was in bed.

They crept downstairs and into the hall, but it was not as late as they thought, and their parents and Aunt Hester and Uncle George were still at the bridge table playing cards!

Father looked up as he heard them, "What are you two doing?"

Abby was so upset. She just wanted to get out quickly before her parents discovered them, but Robert shouted, "Father, come quick! There is a light in Allen's house, and Abby thinks it is the robbers."

"What do you mean, Abby thinks?" Father demanded as all the grownups got up quickly from the table to look out the front window.

"Don't let them see you, or they may get away, " Abby cried.

"O.K., let's go." said Uncle George. "I'll go around to the back door, and Samuel, you take the front. Robert, you come along and watch from the street."

"I'll call the police," Mother said, and then she frowned and exclaimed, "We've no phone…I can't! Never mind, I'll run next door and use their phone."

They all started to run out the front door and Abby followed Robert. Father turned and saw her, "Abby you stay here!"

Abby's feelings were mixed. She wanted to go along, and yet she felt so afraid.

And then it seemed like everything happened at once. The police sirens wailing and the red lights flashing as the squad cars came roaring out. And the men rushing out of the back door with Uncle George right after them and they ran right into Father. Abby ran across the street. She just couldn't stay on the porch!

The police handcuffed the two men and put them into the police car and then came to talk to Father and Abby. It was Abby who told them where the stolen things were hidden and that these were the two men she and Mary Margaret had seen.

After the police had left everyone went back into the house. Abby's heart was still pounding, and even though it was cold outside, Uncle George and Father were sweating, and even Mother looked breathless.

Father put his arms around Abby as he said, "Abigail, you were a tremendous help both in bringing the money from Uncle Mike and in proving his good intentions in helping us. We need to apologize to Mike and to thank him."

Mother and Father went out to the playhouse to find Uncle Mike, but Abby knew he wasn't there.

Uncle Mike didn't come back to the playhouse again. But Abby knew in her heart that he would get his new suit, and when he got the job as a salesman, he would come back.